Praise for
Predictable Magic

"*Predictable Magic* provides a much-needed set of insights, case studies, and methodologies for product design and development. In particular, the products and services being developed for customers in emerging markets must think about design and experience in the way described by *Predictable Magic* if they are to succeed and improve the lives of millions around the world."

—**Nishith Acharya**, Executive Director, The Deshpande Foundation

"An indispensable resource for anyone concerned with creating value through innovation. The EMPOWER framework uniquely combines concepts of creativity, strategy, and psychology in a pragmatic and integrated approach. With concrete cases, it offers many timely insights that can be readily adopted by any organization striving to connect emotionally with its customers. Deepa and Ravi have demystified the black box of creativity."

—**Dr. Arvind Bhambri**, Faculty Director,
Marshall School of Business–Executive Education

"As the competitive playing field shifts from segments to clusters, consumers to cocreators, functionalities to user experiences, and product innovations to new categories, companies are challenged to relate ever more directly with the market's new Big Kahuna—the whole person. How does a large, engineered business system engage an individual's heart and mind and deliver unanticipated benefit? *Predictable Magic* offers a truly elegant answer. Prahalad and Sawhney's EMPOWER framework is practicable, tested, and intuitive. Rely on it: The hours spent with this book will empower your strategy."

—**Jeb Brugmann**, Founding Partner, The Next Practice;
author, *Welcome to the Urban Revolution: How Cities Are Changing the World*

"Prahalad and Sawhney are among the very few designers who understand that meaning itself is a design—that humans are not built into the environment via instinct. *Predictable Magic* demonstrates an appreciation of humans, in all their authenticity, as beauty incarnate: full of asymmetry, paradox, and irony. Prahalad and Sawhney are exceptional product designers, because they are creators of things that allow people to emotionally connect with what is latent in them and deeply personal. A bigger gift no one can offer."

—**Dr. Bob Deutsch**, Cognitive Anthropologist;
President and Founder, Brain Sells

"*Predictable Magic* places the consumer experience at the center of product design and marketing. Empathy and emotions, understood through the concept of persona, bring a richer and fresher perspective on consumer-driven innovation than any other book I have seen. This book is a 'must-read' for anyone concerned with developing products and experiences consumers will love. It provides practical advice, frameworks, and tools to foster successful innovation, without ever falling in the recipe mode."

—**Yves Doz**, The Timken Chaired Professor of Global Technology
and Innovation, INSEAD; author (with Mikko Kosonen), *Fast Strategy*

"By putting the empowerment of people at the center of strategy creation, *Predictable Magic* is as much a book about values and leadership as it is about design. It can help executives find meaning and value in their work as they create meaning and value for their consumers."

—**Dr. Marshall Goldsmith**, world-renowned executive coach; author, *The New York Times* bestsellers, *MOJO* and *What Got You Here Won't Get You There*

"Prahalad and Sawhney shine a light on an important piece of the strategic puzzle: how to convert consumer emotions into successful designs. They provide a rigorous approach to guide innovation efforts from strategy creation through execution. This is a must-read for anyone who is trying to create a new product or develop a new business model."

—**Dr. Vijay Govindarajan**, Earl C. Daum 1924 Professor of International Business, Tuck School of Business, Dartmouth College; Chief Innovation Consultant, GE; author (with Chris Trimble), *Ten Rules for Strategic Innovators*

"Truly great designs are magical—they surprise us with their unexpected functionality, delight us with their thoughtful ergonomics and beguile us with their seductive aesthetics. While every company *strives* to create products and services that dazzle, few achieve this feat. Now, in *Predictable Magic*, Deepa Prahalad and Ravi Sawhney lay out a simple but powerful methodology for turning deep consumer insights into attention-grabbing, expectation-defying designs. If you're looking to increase the 'magic quotient' in the things your company makes and sells, you'll want to dig into *Predictable Magic*."

—**Dr. Gary Hamel**, Visiting Professor, London Business School; author, *The Future of Management* and *Leading the Revolution*

"Prahalad and Sawhney have developed the most comprehensive book I have found on the emerging study of emotional connections between consumers and products. The Psycho-Aesthetics® concept is something that every person who has a leadership role in brand building, product development, or innovation must absorb and understand. *Predictable Magic* is attainable and needs to be integrated into the business architecture of every business."

—**Charles L. Jones**, Vice President, Global Consumer Design, Whirlpool Corporation

"*Predictable Magic* convincingly argues that design is intrinsic to successful product innovation in the consumer marketplace, requiring deep understanding of the emotional and psychological needs and experiential responses of diverse individual consumers, and early integration into the formulation of business strategy. Its engaging verbal and visual exposition draws from many disciplines and distills original insights from the compelling experience of well-chosen case studies into a systematic framework of general applicability in the process of strategic innovation."

—**Dr. Linda Lim**, Professor of Strategy, Ross School of Business, University of Michigan

PREDICTABLE MAGIC

PREDICTABLE MAGIC

Unleash the Power of Design Strategy to Transform Your Business

DEEPA PRAHALAD AND RAVI SAWHNEY

Vice President, Publisher: Tim Moore
Associate Publisher and Director of Marketing: Amy Neidlinger
Wharton Editor: Steve Kobrin
Executive Editor: Jeanne Glasser
Editorial Assistant: Myesha Graham
Operations Manager: Gina Kanouse
Senior Marketing Manager: Julie Phifer
Publicity Manager: Laura Czaja
Assistant Marketing Manager: Megan Colvin
Cover Designer: Hojin Choi
Managing Editor: Kristy Hart
Project Editor: Anne Goebel
Copy Editor: Apostrophe Editing Services
Proofreader: Sheri Cain
Senior Indexer: Cheryl Lenser
Senior Compositor: Gloria Schurick
Manufacturing Buyer: Dan Uhrig

© 2011 by Pearson Education, Inc.
Publishing as Wharton School Publishing
Upper Saddle River, New Jersey 07458

Wharton School Publishing offers excellent discounts on this book when ordered in quantity for bulk purchases or special sales. For more information, please contact U.S. Corporate and Government Sales, 1-800-382-3419, corpsales@pearsontechgroup.com. For sales outside the U.S., please contact International Sales at international@pearson.com.

Printed in the United States of America

Second Printing September 2010

ISBN-10 0-13-702348-0
ISBN-13 978-0-13-702348-6

Pearson Education LTD.
Pearson Education Australia PTY, Limited.
Pearson Education Singapore, Pte. Ltd.
Pearson Education North Asia, Ltd.
Pearson Education Canada, Ltd.
Pearson Educación de Mexico, S.A. de C.V.
Pearson Education—Japan
Pearson Education Malaysia, Pte. Ltd.

Library of Congress Cataloging-in-Publication Data:

Prahalad, Deepa, 1972-
  Predictable magic: unleash the power of design strategy to transform your business / Deepa Prahalad, Ravi Sawhney.
     p. cm.
  ISBN 978-0-13-702348-6 (hardcover : alk. paper) 1. Strategic planning. 2. Technological innovations. 3. Competition. I. Sawhney, Ravi, 1956- II. Title.
  HD30.28.P7 2011
  658.4'012—dc22
                                             2009054414

For my parents, who taught me to ask questions and look for answers with persistence and compassion
Deepa Prahalad

For my parents, who instilled in me the need for integrity and caring for others
Ravi Sawhney

Contents

Acknowledgments

This book would not have been possible without the generosity of collaborators who offered their energy, insight, and encouragement. We are grateful for their input and certain that this book has been enriched by their contributions.

Our editors at Pearson, Jeanne Glasser, Steve Kobrin, and Tim Moore, were willing to take on two new authors and guide us patiently through the process of bringing this book to life. We were also able to gain the insights of many people who we have collaborated with when they agreed to be interviewed for this project. Special thanks are due to John Herrington (of Amana, and now LG), Robert Hayman of Discus Dental, Simon Jones of JBL (now of Line 6), Eric Barnes and Paul Shustak of KOR Water, Dave Mason from RKS Guitars, Hardy Steinman of Zyliss, Wayne Ludlum of VestaLife, and Simon Fleming-Wood of Pure Digital Technologies for ensuring that the perspective of executives came through in the chapters. We also benefited from our dialogue with Dr. Bob Deutsch, Dr. Chip Wood, Tom Matano, Dale Jensen, and Frank Tyneski for their insights on design and its business relevance.

Every individual at RKS has contributed to this effort at some stage. We cannot adequately thank the team at RKS for their dedication and hard work, on the projects that are featured in this book. All of the RKS team members over the years have built the foundation of the firm and consistently produced award-winning work and generated bottom-line results for our clients. Lance Hussey, Chris Glupker, and Kurt Botsai were early employees of RKS, and almost every project has been touched by them as they have helped to shape and evolve the practice of Psycho-Aesthetics®. They shared my vision early on and continually pushed themselves to execute and rose to the occasion as we took on more ambitious projects. Over the course of this project, everyone we called on put in efforts that went beyond our requests or the call of duty. Barb Mackintosh and Karen Kelly provided their sharp editorial eyes, keen insights, and well-reasoned critiques to each version of the chapters. Hojin Choi developed early cover concepts and the inspiring final design. Several of the designers, especially Harnish Jani, Leah Thomas, and Eric Lai created the illustrations that help to bring concepts to life throughout the book. The title of *Predictable Magic* was adapted from our former colleague, Tom White. Our conversations with Lance Hussey, Harnish Jani, and Ingvald Smith-Kielland yielded many of the insights reflected within the chapters.

Design is a multidisciplinary effort, and much of our learning comes from outside our organization—and profession. The foundations of Psycho-Aesthetics were inspired by the work of Abraham Maslow, whose keen understanding of human behavior and motivation has led to many of our most inspired designs. As the design profession has evolved and matured, communication with consumers has grown in importance, and philosopher Joseph Campbell has helped us to discover the stories and narratives that have enabled us to connect in a meaningful way. We have always believed that design is more than an aesthetic challenge, but a business challenge as well. Readers will easily recognize the inspiration from leading thinkers in business strategy including Peter Drucker, C.K. Prahalad, Gary Hamel, Michael Porter, W. Chan Kim, Renée Mauborgne, and Yves Doz.

It is an exciting time to be in the design profession, and the work of other firms and individuals has certainly provided inspiration in pushing the limits of where design can be applied and to refine our methodology. As always, the support and help of the Industrial Designer's Society of America (IDSA) has been firm as we have tried to stake new ground. The design profession is composed of a diverse lot of talented individuals, and many small firms who have been steadily helping companies and entrepreneurs bring their ideas to market. We draw tremendous inspiration from their work and hope that this book empowers them in their creative endeavors.

We do not speak about the potential for business and design to work effectively together on a theoretical basis. Our collaboration with business schools and our own entrepreneurial efforts inform our recommendations. We are especially grateful to Rajib Adhikary and Elie Ofek who introduced us to Harvard Business School; this resulted in a HBS Case study of RKS Guitars and Psycho-Aesthetics.

Harvard and other schools, notably USC, UCLA, and Pepperdine, have regularly invited us to speak about the method in their classes. The team who worked on producing RKS Guitars and my partner Dave Mason also deserve mention. Linda Tischler of *Fast Company* generously provided us the opportunity to blog and share our stories with a wider business audience.

Of course, our families, friends, and mentors provide the support to venture into new areas and are what really sustain us as we take on new roles. For both of us, the love and encouragement of parents, spouses, siblings, and children have made this effort worthwhile. Both of us have had professional mentors and teachers who helped shape our worldviews.

Deepa Prahalad

My parents (C.K. and Gayatri Prahalad) have always been my biggest inspiration and support. They not only believed in me, but also listened to me prattle on about design and debated with me. My brother and his family (Murali, Punam, and Nithya Prahalad) were steadfast in their support. My in-laws, Anand and Shaila Abhyankar, always offered their encouragement. My extended family all over the globe dutifully checked in throughout the process. However, it was my husband, Ashwin Abhyankar, and son Arjun who indulged me with tremendous patience and good humor, adjusted their lives around deadlines, and made sure I could devote time and attention to work. They were generous with their affection and support, and enabled me to keep plugging away.

While a student at the University of Michigan, I had the benefit of learning about the world from great professors such as Ken Lieberthal, Linda Lim, Jeff Winters, and Pradeep Chhibber. All of them helped me to build an awareness of the many moving parts in every situation and instilled a healthy skepticism of the "obvious" answer. At the Tuck School of Business, I learned from professors such as Vijay Govindarajan, Sidney Finkelstein, and Richard D'Aveni. Professionally, my experience with Cargill in Singapore and with Safe-Med in San Diego provided me with real-world insights that I continue to draw on.

Ravi Sawhney

My wife Amalia supported and encouraged me in this effort; always believing in me. My parents Ved and Lajya, my brother Ramesh, and sister Parmela, shared my excitement. My daughters Nesha and Sita, my son-in-law Ingvald, and stepchildren Ben and Claire lent their enthusiasm.

My mentor Dick Bruton inspired me to forge ahead and become an industrial designer at a time I was about to abandon my major in industrial design. Leroy Petersen's mastery of ceramics taught me how to combine form and function. The very special, late Hollis Killen who I met as a teacher when I was 12 and stayed friends with for almost 40 years set me on my professional path. Sunil Dhir first encouraged me to start RKS. Both Sunil and Daniel Frank have been trusted friends and advisors through the years.

The example of Alan Kay who changed the world though his work remains a huge inspiration. I was privileged enough to help develop some of his concepts into the first touch-screen interface while part of the team at Xerox. The understandings and insights developed there in the late '70s started my investigations and innovations in the psyche and of user interaction reflected in *Predictable Magic*.

It is from a very privileged position that we can therefore both speak about emotional connections and their value. We understand their importance through our families, friends, and colleagues and know their power to transform organizations and the lives of individuals.

Deepa Prahalad
Ravi Sawhney
Thousand Oaks, CA
December 2009

About the Authors

Deepa Prahalad holds a BA in Political Science and Economics from the University of Michigan and an MBA from the Tuck School of Business at Dartmouth. Passionate about emerging markets and innovation, she began her career researching how to increase efficiency in UN procurement and later moved to Singapore to become a commodities trader with Cargill.

Deepa's career has also included work as a management consultant specializing in the opportunities at the intersection of consumer experiences, technology, and strategy. She collaborated with RKS to research and co-author *Predictable Magic*, and is the creator of the EMPOWER framework.

Ravi Sawhney is president and CEO of RKS, a global leader in Strategy, Innovation, and Design. Founded in 1980, RKS has incubated companies, created licensed products, and won more than 80 design awards for clients ranging from start-ups to large multinational corporations.

Ravi invented Psycho-Aesthetics, the popular design strategy which has been the subject of a Harvard Business School Case Study. The Academy of Art University in San Francisco awarded Ravi an honorary doctorate for his body of work, the development of Psycho-Aesthetics, and the reinvention of the electric guitar with RKS Guitar's open architecture guitar. Ravi has been named on more than 150 patents, in the United States and worldwide. He also serves as an expert design blogger, sharing his insights on Fastcompany.com. In 2009, Ravi was elected as an IDSA (Industrial Designers Society of America) Fellow.

Preface

Why Psycho-Aesthetics?

Psycho-Aesthetics is the RKS process of creating emotional connections between consumers and designs. It spans the spectrum from research to strategy to implementation and finally to consumer experience. By revealing the triggers that attract buyers, generate the purchase impulse, and create emotional connection, this process can empower you to build the viral demand that leads to segment leadership. Whether you're a business leader, or engaged in strategy, innovation, and design in any way, Psycho-Aesthetics can help achieve your goals.

To understand the roots of this design thinking methodology, we simply need look at the psychology of what it means to be human, from the most basic elements we require for survival on through to the need for positive self-image and affirmation. When survival needs have been satisfied, we seek to satisfy our needs to grow and evolve…to adorn ourselves and our surroundings and to augment our being. The ongoing quest to satisfy these needs is the root of consumerism.

The days of simply designing a better (or bigger or prettier) mousetrap have passed. Consumers around the world have evolved into design and experience critics. Today, designs, services, and experiences must do much more than fill basic needs…they must connect emotionally. By understanding the core of human psyche and how it is an essential part of consumerism, we can all create that connection, that "wow" factor that makes people want to spread the joy of their discovery. When we get this connection right, it's pure magic.

Psycho-Aesthetics is a highly visual way of approaching these challenges. It's a scalable set of tools that enables mapping of the consumer audience, competitive products, and brands. When these market "windows" are aligned, consumers with unmet needs can be clearly recognized. We can then develop strategy, design, and storytelling to reach them. The result is tangible, memorable experiences and connections that build brand loyalty.

This methodology can allow you to look into the hearts and minds of markets. And after you have, you can clearly understand how and why to attract, engage, trigger adoption, and cause the viral effects on the market that most companies only dream of. What's more, you can use this process to generate the desired results repeatedly and predictably.

So, whether you're an Apple or you're selling apples on the corner, Psycho-Aesthetics can and will show you how to create higher levels of adoption, greater levels of perceived value, and, most important, create consumers that feel so good about your business, the experience, and themselves that they simply have to spread the word.

With these tools, you too can create Predictable Magic.

Introduction

"Information's pretty thin stuff unless mixed with experience."
—Clarence Day

This book is the result of a collaboration that grew out of a chance meeting. Although as individuals we have followed different professional paths, we quickly found common ground in two fervently shared beliefs: in the power of innovation and in the importance of the individual. The road to those convictions was different for each of us, but debating how these ideals may shape both design and strategy has been a source of tremendous learning and growth.

It's the Individual That Matters

For almost 30 years, one of us, Ravi, has been leading RKS Design, the firm he founded. As an industrial designer and entrepreneur, Ravi has been involved in the innovation process in many industries from concept to execution. As the scope and volume of projects grew, so too did the need to efficiently and reliably understand the needs of the clients, market, and end users. To make sense of design success and failure, Ravi drew on experience in the heydays at Xerox during the 1970s working on some of the first versions of the modern touch screen to understand how human behavior relates to design and design to experience. Reflecting on hours of consumer testing, he realized that most of the lackluster performers (in technology and

1

elsewhere) did not have functional flaws—they simply failed to engage consumers. Some products made people feel inferior, as if they didn't understand great design. Others intimidated the audience, such as the early versions of the touch screen.

Puzzling over how to prevent this scenario led to a long process of exploration and the development of Psycho-Aesthetics®, the RKS philosophy of emotionally connecting with consumers through design. The focus of this approach is squarely on the individuals, specifically their emotions, aspirations, and connections as the starting point for strategy and design. Tracking the individual experience and emotional response is the goal of the process, rather than creating new functions and features alone. The test of success lies in whether the design empowers individuals and creates a meaningful experience.

For one of us, Deepa, business strategy and innovation are more than a matter of business school and professional experience; they are somewhat of an inheritance. Her father, C.K. Prahalad, was a professor at the University of Michigan Business School, and she had the benefit of watching, and often participating, in robust debates at the dinner table with MBA students, CEOs, and academics. Many of these sketches and diagrams created during these gatherings eventually entered the market and became hugely successful products and services. The idea that business should have a tangible impact on improving the lives of individuals—providing both opportunity and value—was cemented early on. Here, too, the role of aspirations—of managers, consumers, and corporations—was seen as the driving force in successful strategy and innovation.

These lessons resonated, though Deepa chose to study political science and economics. The Berlin Wall fell and Tiananmen Square unfolded while she was in high school, and the Soviet Union imploded a few days before a final exam in Cold War politics during her sophomore year in college. During her first "real" job (based in Singapore), her company and most others were working on strategies to enter the newly liberalizing markets of India and China. Many offerings that had been successful in the West were promptly rejected, even when prices were competitive. Although people were hungry for change, they also wanted to retain a connection to their own cultures and beliefs. Here, too, the voices of individuals and their emotions made themselves known, loud and clear.

The Model

Businesses today must respond to rising consumer aspirations. We wrote this book in the hope that understanding how to make these the starting point for strategy can help both the business and design communities transform their good intentions and need for self-sustenance into the enduring businesses that create opportunity for themselves and others. Executives, too, are empowered when their work has a positive impact on the world around them. We hope that this cycle can serve to counter the cynicism that abounds and help steer the path to solutions.

This book narrates some of the cases from the evolving practice of Psycho-Aesthetics. We firmly believe that innovation is as possible for a two-person start-up as for a large diversified corporation. We chose cases that represent a range of industries and challenges. They are largely based on our own experience. However, that choice is not meant to negate the truly outstanding achievements of other design firms and many innovative companies. The cases included herein were chosen merely because these were the ones that we could narrate with authenticity and a level of detail that may help you and your teams as they undertake similar challenges.

Highlighting the role of emotional insight should not take away from the importance of data and research. We simply believe that the legitimate need for structure and process should also explicitly capture the emotion and experience of the consumer. These are the ultimate measures of market success and need to be considered along with financial analyses. Better yet, the tools are accessible to those who are in charge of actually implementing design and innovation—the designers and executives themselves. In acknowledgment of the time and resource constraints in most firms, the process is clear, efficient, and replicable.

Roger Martin, Dean of the Rottman School and a vocal advocate of design, once commented, "Strategists don't have to learn how to understand designers better. In the future, they will have to become designers."[1] We show how the energy directed into creating quantitative metrics of emotions and cognitive experience can be understood in the early stages, reducing risks of error and creating sustainable company business models in the process. Today, Psycho-Aesthetics goes way beyond product design, enabling businesses to look beyond the horizon. That's another reason the book is called *Predictable Magic*—not only does Psycho-Aesthetics empower businesses to create magic predictably, but it also enables us to predict what designs and brand strategies will be successful in the future.

A Simpler Way to Innovate and Design

In this book, we share the Psycho-Aesthetics philosophy and methodology through case studies from various industries. We start with helping to answer some of the basic questions about design: How should you approach the design process? How do you know when you've arrived at the right solution? And how can you make sure that your design and business strategies work together—consistently? We then show you how to translate these insights into actual products and services. You can

- Learn how to map existing products, consumers, and channels using the Psycho-Aesthetics methodology to reveal new opportunities for innovation
- Understand how to identify design features that can enable you to emotionally connect with your consumers

- Mitigate risk by understanding your consumers and setting appropriate design priorities
- Learn, with fresh cases, how companies from Fortune 500 to start-ups have used design to create sustained organic growth
- Align *all* stakeholders around the design process

It is now widely understood that consumers engage for emotional reasons and adopt based on rich and fulfilling experience. Yet few companies look at emotion and experience explicitly as a starting point for strategy and design. We have found that those willing to do so often see higher profits, brand value, and levels of consumer satisfaction.

About This Book

This book is organized in two parts. **Part I, "Creation of a Design Strategy,"** focuses on aligning creative and executive teams and creating an actionable manifest that is the basis of successful design. Teams are guided to answer three major questions in creating a design strategy and use Psycho-Aesthetics mapping techniques and tools to guide the collaboration.

Part II, "Implementation and Consumer Experience," covers the topics of implementation and consumer experience. Here, the process of translating insights and strategy into physical design are discussed along with some litmus tests for design success. We discuss how to position these designs in real-life retail and Web settings so that the value of the offering is easily understood and communicated to the consumer.

We ask and answer some familiar strategic questions about markets, consumers and opportunities, but we answer them from the perspective of the consumer—not the firm. Understanding that all insight would not be "provable analysis," we sought to make the decision-making logic transparent by mapping consumer interactions in a collaborative setting. This represents the culmination of lessons learned from across industries, which have shown us time and time again that there are basic emotional responses that apply to all consumer behaviors, and these responses can be analyzed objectively. We have broken down the steps into a framework we call "EMPOWER." Empowerment is after all, what the best companies must do for their teams inside, and what they must do for their consumers as well.

We invite you to continue the conversation with us at www.predictablemagic.com.

Part I

Creation of a Design Strategy

1

Set the Stage for Success

Designing the Intangible

Bubble gum. Teddy bears. Legos. Roller skates. Red lipstick. Sports cars. All of these transcend the boundaries between object and experience. At each stage of life, designs become part of our lives and the stories we tell ourselves and those around us. They resonate with us emotionally.

Observing this phenomenon is much easier than creating it. There is no shortage of corporate attention and resources directed toward understanding the needs and desires of consumers. Despite these efforts, most new offerings fail to connect with consumers, and hordes of supposedly "satisfied" consumers defect. Without a consistent emotional connection, there is no brand connection—no barrier to defection. Worse still, the cost and visibility of these failures is increasing. However, the market performance of the success stories (such as the iPod) and the excitement generated by compelling new concepts provide a convincing case for the power of design to capture our imagination—and produce impressive returns in the process. For this reason, many companies today are integrating design thinking into their cultures at higher levels. This is an important shift in mindset, but the success of these efforts depends on the degree to which insights can be translated into strategy and action.

New Rules of Competition

Today, firms in all industries find themselves *competing on design*. The concept of design has broadened beyond the purely aesthetic and now includes every aspect of the consumer's interaction and experience with the brand.

Companies invest vast resources into innovation and strategy. They hire market researchers, consultants, and armies of internal staff to identify new opportunities and develop new concepts. Yet the results are less than encouraging: Some studies suggest that 70 percent of strategies never get executed and more than 80 percent of new product introductions fail or underperform. Of course, there are visible exceptions in the most crowded and competitive industries such as Apple (computing) and Target (discount retail). The companies that manage to innovate successfully enjoy financial rewards *and* the respect and affection of consumers. These successes depend on carefully integrating corporate strategy with design to forge deep, emotional connections.

These emotional connections are the little-understood magic that can transform a product from an object that simply serves a purpose into a rewarding and empowering experience. By creating these connections, design transforms business strategy into business success.

In *Predictable Magic*, we seek to demystify the design process to make strategy and design more understandable and pragmatic. Something you can use and profit from. In this way, we can transform what for many is a black art into a repeatable process. Psycho-Aesthetics® is the RKS philosophy of creating emotional connections between consumers and designs. It spans the spectrum from research to strategy to implementation and finally to consumer experience. This process harnesses your knowledge and creativity and cultivates them into results. To put it simply, Psycho-Aesthetics takes the magic out of the process and puts it into the consumer experience.

Those on the front lines leading innovation know the importance of balancing inspiration with execution. Design is an increasingly important ingredient in carrying out strategy and can also be a powerful tool for mitigating the risk inherent in bringing innovations to market.

A New Perspective on Design

Psycho-Aesthetics arose as a formal practice out of the study of designs that were lauded for their beauty but failed in the market. Careful analyses reveal a simple and profound truth:

"It's not how you feel about the design, it's how it makes you feel about yourself."

This counterintuitive idea has major implications for how companies approach their study of consumers and the innovation process. Few consumers buy purely on the basis of need. In the developed world, a majority of purchases are driven by a need for entertainment and self-actualization. But even for the four billion people in the world who remain poor, aspirations play a pivotal role in their consumption decisions—note the size and growth of the cell phone industry in emerging markets.

When we look at design success across industries, it's clear that the relationship between what catches our attention and what eventually wins our hearts can be mysterious and complex. Consider some of the brands in different categories that are consistently given top ratings from consumers—from airlines (Jet Blue, Southwest), cars (BMW, Honda, Toyota), and food (Costco, Trader Joe's, and Wegman's), to Internet businesses (Amazon, eBay, and Google).[1] There isn't a pattern to the functionality, aesthetics, or price points in their offerings. But there is a consistency to their quality and the unique and consistent experience they provide—in short, in the way that they tend to the well being of their consumers.

Of course, there is no shortage of alternatives for the specific products and services that the top brands provide. It is the way they respond to the emotional needs of consumers that sets them apart. The ultimate goal of design is not merely making things that people enjoy or creating awareness of the company. When design creates feelings of empowerment, people are eager to share their experience with others. This cycle is essential to generating demand virally and building brand loyalty.

Overcoming the Hurdles

The importance of creating emotional connections comes as no surprise for business leaders engaged in the strategy, innovation, and design process. Regardless of organizational function, those involved with creating new concepts or taking ideas to market are likely to find themselves frustrated in confronting two major hurdles:

- **Information overload**—There is no efficient way to process and prioritize the volumes of data and research that exist in most corporations today. The market research industry is estimated at a staggering $19 billion[2] as consumer behavior and demographics can be studied in exhaustive detail. However, the vast majority of consumer purchase decisions are made on an emotional basis and experts estimate that up to 95 percent of buying behavior originates at a subconscious level.[3]

  Although information is abundant, *insight* can be in short supply. Traditional market research reveals very little about the consumer's *emotional* triggers in the decision process in a way that can inform design and strategy.

- **Inadequate models for collaboration**—Even in the most enlightened organizations, fostering collaboration between executive and creative teams brings special challenges. The differences in tools, education, and perspective frequently lead to delays, battles, unsatisfying compromises, and uninspired results. However, companies that find ways to resolve these issues can create an important source of competitive advantage.

As a design firm, we have had a unique vantage point in this debate. We have collaborated with companies in many industries for almost 30 years. At its best, design is an excellent method for creating organic growth, brand awareness, and meaningful consumer experiences. It also remains one of the most underleveraged tools in many organizations. We knew that we wanted to do more than help firms create one-time product success. Helping clients build brands for the long term requires understanding how to build and operationalize consumer insights and demands by developing an efficient collaborative process to enable repeatable success.

But that does not mean that companies looking to understand and incorporate design need to upend everything that they know. Sweeping corporate reorganization is not always a realistic (or effective) option, especially when a company is engaged with maintaining its competitive position. Moreover, changing the course of strategy and the inner workings of companies are not areas that design firms were traditionally consulted on. Therefore, the tools that we developed to lead innovation do not rely on a given corporate culture or executive champion. They are also not dependent on complex financial modeling. Psycho-Aesthetics guides the design process by creating dialogue and collaboration among stakeholders and empathy for the consumer.

Predictable Magic shows those interested in driving change how to move beyond brainstorming and create the consumer insight and collaboration needed to achieve breakthrough success—no matter your industry or company size.

Psycho-Aesthetics: An Integrated Approach to Innovation and Design

Confronting two of the major challenges in the design process—creating rich, actionable consumer insight and fostering more effective collaboration—led to the development of Psycho-Aesthetics. This framework makes it possible to systematically understand the emotional reactions of consumers to products, services, and experiences.

Just like the consumer marketplace, new tools and concepts have to connect with the stakeholders they are designed for...Capturing data and intuition in one place is a goal that remains elusive in most firms. Spreadsheets get updated far more often than assumptions about consumer behavior. Through our work with large corporations and entrepreneurial firms, we saw how business decisions about branding, channels, and pricing could weaken the impact of new concepts. The need for aligning strategy and design became obvious. Strategy without design is just good research. Design without strategy is just a good idea.

The case studies we share here span the range from start-ups to long-established, well-known firms. They are meant as an illustration of how to use emotional insight to guide the design process and to show the framework in practice across a wide range of industries. However, a single great design will not create lasting business success. Nor are we making the case that design can save a dying category or overcome inadequate funding, lack of corporate support, or flawed business models. Many good designs are quickly dismissed, and the best ones are quickly copied. Companies therefore need to innovate constantly to stay on top, and a predictable process for doing so can dramatically increase the odds of success. We know that the design process can be made more collaborative (for all stakeholders), efficient, and consistent with the right tools. And when design and strategy work well together, it can create new categories, transform industries, and drive financial results.

Psycho-Aesthetics is compelling because it creates efficiency in a complex undertaking—understanding the consumer. Technology has enabled the collection of large amounts of trend data. The problem is, all this data and measurement can create *analysis paralysis* in which companies cannot turn information into actionable insights. Measuring everything doesn't create insight any more than eating everything creates health. This methodology enables executives and designers to zero in on the data that matters because it gives them a means to create a compelling consumer experiences.

The Importance of Emotion—and Action

Our experience shows that anticipating and responding to consumer *emotions*, rather than parsing demographics and focusing on market research, has proven to be the most reliable indicator of design success. Developing a simple, intuitive process for incorporating this emotional insight into the design process has involved vigorous experimentation. Over time, we discovered that factoring in emotion has not made design more complex but introduced clarity to the decisions and trade-offs that come with implementation. That clarity has enabled us to breathe new life into stale categories, help companies climb back from decline, and enter the market and seize share, faster, with more lasting results than we dared to hope for.

What does this mean in practical terms? How can a firm begin to practice this philosophy? What are the resources and skills involved in implementation? Based on our work with diverse clients, we have distilled the process into distinct phases that can be easily remembered with the acronym **EMPOWER**. The Psycho-Aesthetics process is a powerful catalyst in empowering clients and design professionals to innovate. Not coincidentally, EMPOWER also describes the experience that we aim to create for consumers. Empowering experiences create connections between consumers and brands. These bonds are the basis of market leadership and sustained financial performance.

> **E**nable Your Stakeholders
> **M**ap the Future
> **P**ersonify Your Consumer
> **O**wn the Opportunity
> **W**ork the Design Process
> **E**ngage Emotionally
> **R**eward Your Consumer

The idea that emotional connections are the real drivers of growth and prosperity seemed radical when we began to use this approach. If the results from objective data can be misleading, it was hardly surprising that business people were once hesitant to base major strategic decisions on *emotional* considerations. But emotional insight translated into design creates real business results. Consider some of the following examples of this philosophy in practice:

- In the mid-1990s, the Minimed insulin pump was a breakthrough technology that unintentionally reinforced the stigma of being a patient. By redesigning it to look like a pager (which were then perceived as "cool" and "hip"), sales went from $45 million to $171 million in 3 years and the firm was acquired by Medtronic for more than $3 billion.

- An appliance engagement with Amana revealed that its products' high quality was not reflected in its styling. Enhancing badging, knobs, and graphics to reflect its brand raised costs by $0.30 but commanded a $100/unit premium at retail. The result was more than $20 million in profits and an acquisition by Maytag.

- Collaboration with Discus Dental to create the Zoom! Tooth Whitening system began more than 2 years after Brite Smile entered the category and began taking market share. Psycho-Aesthetics was used to design all components of the professional tooth whitening experience (from the syringe to the whitening lamp). Today, Zoom! sells more than 100,000 of the patented syringes per week and ultimately acquired Brite Smile Professional to secure its market position.

Looking at design as a means to deliver empowerment was central to all these efforts. The credibility of many companies today rests on whether they actually deliver value to consumers as they produce profits. In an increasingly global marketplace, few opportunities can be understood with financial metrics alone (although these will always be an important measure). Many of these markets and new consumers can be better understood—and designed for—through a deep understanding of their needs, desires, and aspirations. In this way, Psycho-Aesthetics can help translate the good intentions of most businesspeople into tangible business results.

The Value of Consumer Emotions (and the High Cost of Ignoring Them)

Though no one denies that consumer emotions and experience are important, many hesitate to leverage them because they seem subjective and difficult to quantify. But take a look at your balance sheet. Consumer emotions are all over the place—implicitly and explicitly. Neglecting to consider emotions and experience for all stakeholders at every stage will always show up on the bottom line.

Intangible value of brands—Brand value is a major component of intangible assets determined by factors such as company reputation and goodwill. These are alternate names for consumer's feelings about a firm. According to some estimates, intangible value now accounts for 62 percent of enterprise value on a global basis.[4] In addition, long-recognized marketing tools such as the lifetime value of a consumer and the value of word-of-mouth marketing can now be quantified in many industries. The link between consumer emotions to the bottom line has become more visible as a result.

Vulnerability of financial modeling—Assume the classic scenario of Company A and Company B. Would you bet on a decision process that is based on observed human behavior and emerging trends or assumptions and historic data? If you voted for the former, you intuitively understand the value of ethnography and "human factors" to supplement the traditional methods of financial modeling.

Increased chances of survival—Few companies have histories that do not include periods of difficulty and decline. It is often during the hard times that the feelings of consumers can make a difference in terms of which companies survive. Call it karma. When Starbucks announced the closing of 600 of its stores due to a poor economy, there were community efforts to "Save Our Starbucks" in many locations. At the same time, some investment banks and retailers with long histories folded with scarcely a protest—and sometimes to cheers. Although the love of consumers can't compensate for poor management or business models, it may afford the flexibility to try out new strategies in good and bad times.

Impact of social networking—What are your consumers saying when they get on YouTube? Twitter? Have they listed themselves as fans of your products on Facebook? Consumers are not only making purchase decisions based on emotion, they are providing feedback the same way. Today, those opinions reach far outside their immediate social network. Most of what people feel and say needs to be positive for your company to thrive.

The poet Maya Angelou once observed, "People forget what you said, they forget what you did, but they never forget how you made them feel." The emotional impact companies have on consumers is perhaps their most lasting legacy...and the largest element of their brand equity. It certainly deserves to be at the forefront of everything the company does.

2

Enable Your Stakeholders

In 2000, Amana, one of America's oldest brands, had a difficult brand revival problem: The company had a quality product that no one seemed to notice. Several major retailers had dropped its appliances, and the company was on the verge of idling one of its plants. It had millions of dollars in consumer research done by leading agencies. After months spent isolating the cause of decline, Amana knew the problem was that its design did not capture consumers' attention. It also discovered that its brand was virtually unknown to a new generation of buyers. Beyond that, it was unsure about how to move forward. John Herrington, the project leader and VP of marketing for Amana, summarized the problem by saying, "We had come to a point where we had men designing appliances that were primarily used by women and we were trying to keep pace with cost-cutting. We were having too many discussions about performance and not enough attention was paid to how the consumer actually interacts with the product...."[1]

Amana was eager to win back consumers and market share. Executives who had invested heavily in creating a quality product were aware that the conversation in the marketplace had changed. Aesthetics and new features were becoming more important to consumers, especially those with larger homes and dedicated laundry rooms. However, redesigning during lean times left little room for error, and speed was a critical consideration.

Amana's story is just one example of a scenario being played out in every industry. Brands and entire categories find themselves in decline despite good quality, functional performance, and competitive pricing. Although all these factors remain important, they are no longer enough to create sustainable growth and build connections with consumers.

New Stakeholders, New Process

Breakthrough design does not happen in a vacuum. It's not something that can be tacked on at the end of the product development process. The complexity of new product introductions, diversity of consumers, and global competition means that far more people in every organization are invested in the design development process. To truly innovate, executives, marketers, engineers, and designers must work in concert from the start. Unfortunately, few business tools focus on creating collaboration among disciplines. Although some large organizations have found ways to break down organizational silos, it remains the exception rather than the rule.

Design involves a deep understanding of the consumer and a clear understanding of business implications of various approaches. Executives often take the blame for being focused on the bottom line at the expense of the consumer, but that is rarely the reason for poor outcomes. If companies weren't interested in listening to consumers, market research would not be a $19 billion dollar industry.[2] Top companies such as Procter & Gamble spend more than $200 million a year studying consumer behavior.[3] It is obvious, however, that endless amount of demographic data, financial projections, and anecdotal information rarely add up to great market insight. In fact, many design *failures* can be traced to an inability to make sense of contradictory information.

Finding a way to enable communication, create consensus, and ultimately build confidence and alignment among stakeholders is critical. Surveys of executives suggest that aligning strategy with consumer experience remains one of the toughest organizational challenges to contend with.[4] Succeeding in this effort requires sustained effort from people with very different ways of looking at the world. Designers work by instinct. Engineers rely on numbers. Executive and marketing decision-makers require a rational basis for their design decisions. Simply bringing together a group of bright individuals and asking them to be open-minded rarely bridges these gaps. We need a methodology to enable effective collaboration.

Why It Doesn't Happen Naturally

Sadly, much of the debate about design and design thinking has centered on playing up the differences between intuitive and rational thinkers, creatives, and "suits" for dramatic effect. This is unfortunate, because both bring vital knowledge and experience and both constituencies must answer to the market. However, there are legitimate reasons why managers and designers can't always communicate effectively. These fall into three main categories:

- **Size and fragmentation of the design industry**— According to the Bureau of Labor Statistics, there are 48,000 commercial and industrial designers in the United States (with an estimated 30 percent of them working independently) and approximately 4,000,000 business professionals including management consultants, market researchers, and top executives. There simply may not have been enough opportunities for these groups to work closely together in the past.

- **Education and training**—Learning styles and education also play a role in communication. Most designers have backgrounds in art and learn through observation and prototyping. Designers can adjust to cost and manufacturing requirements, but they often rely on intuition and subjective aesthetic sensibilities that can be difficult to translate into business terms. Engineering professionals are, by nature, very methodical and practical, whereas executives and marketing managers need to understand demographics, market factors, and the bottom line.

- **History**—In the not-so-distant past, designers were brought in when strategy—or even a nearly finished product—was already in place. The design effort focused on aesthetics to enhance an existing product. Today, the conversation is not just about *how* to design something, but about *what* to design. Companies have realized that design needs to be involved from the start, but processes for doing so effectively are few.

Essential Ingredients for Alignment

Several key elements are required for teams to move beyond these barriers to consensus building. The answer to breaking through the clutter doesn't require more research, data, or spreadsheets. It requires reorienting priorities. Consumers, after all, don't make decisions based on the same criteria as companies do. Their purchase behavior and loyalty is largely guided by emotion. Tuning into their decision-making process can help all parties understand the larger context of the marketplace. Aligning stakeholders requires these essentials:

- **Establishing a common language**—Collaboration among stakeholders is still hindered by the language barriers between departments and teams. In international summits, headphones for simultaneous translation are a common sight. The complexity of the issues involved—disarmament, climate change, and terrorism—already make resolutions difficult. If the stakeholders didn't have the ability to hear the arguments in their own language, the consensus required to move forward would simply not happen.

  Although the situation inside most companies is not quite so dire, the direction of the company is often at stake. Stakeholders need tools to communicate effectively and efficiently about what matters to the consumer. Rather than employing teams of unseen "translators," a highly visual approach is needed to overcome these challenges.

- **Quantifying emotional demands**—At first blush, emotions seem too complex and hard to pin down. How can you possibly rate or value one emotion over another? The solution can be found in studying how consumers change in response to their circumstances. It's an elemental part of the human psyche that we must first meet our most basic needs—safety, security, shelter. We need these to survive. But as each level of needs is met, consumers evolve, aspiring to become more. To be loved, to feel validated, to become empowered. These needs can be identified and understood in ways that resonate with all stakeholders.

- **Visualizing as a means to success**—Quantification helps executives and engineers incorporate emotions into decisions, but numbers alone don't speak to designers. Mapping the emotions and interactivity levels (covered in detail in Chapter 3, "Map the Future") speaks to both left- and right-brained stakeholders. When consumer, product, and brand maps are aligned, the clear market opportunity is revealed. When the common goal becomes clear in this way, the team can move beyond mere alignment into laser-focused action.

- **Mobilizing the brain trust through inclusion**—The most critical task in the early phases of most projects is to capture the implicit knowledge of the team involved in implementation. After the completion of the appliance projects, John Herrington, the project leader from VP of Marketing for Amana, reflected on his experience with this methodology: "Our success with the process was as much about including people as anything else. If we hadn't done this and had an identical strategy, I'm still not convinced that we would have been able to implement it...." Trying to rally the troops around an idea after the concept has been developed rarely works. Reversing this process—mobilizing the troops to develop the idea—is a far more effective and efficient approach. Providing a context for stakeholders to see their data and expertise in the context of consumers' emotional responses is the backbone of successful collaboration and design.

Why Visualization Matters

"I'll know it when I see it." This truism applies not only to products and services, but also increasingly to strategy. Our ability to "know it when we see it" does not mean we're relying on instinct over intellectual rigor. Our senses—and *especially* our eyes—play a vital role in abstract reasoning and inform our perceptions, often without us realizing it. The conscious bandwidth of all our senses is much smaller than the actual total, as shown in Figure 2.1.

Consumers make decisions in a split second, whether or not they want to. Interdisciplinary teams are also more likely to internalize and implement a strategy that is represented visually than if the same information comes to them in a report. The benefits to using highly visual tools are profound.

Processing Capacity of Different Senses	Total Bandwith (Bits / Seconds)	Conscious Bandwith (Bits / Seconds)
Sight	10,000,000	40
Hearing	100,000	30
Touch	1,000,000	5
Taste	1,000	1
Smell	100,000	1

© RKS Design

Figure 2.1   Bandwidth of all the senses

Process in Action—Amana

In Amana's case, everyone was committed to doing what they thought was important—and the result was an emphasis on quality. However, the singular focus on performance failed to take into consideration the design factors needed for consumers to make an emotional connection with the product. This contributed to consumers' lack of interest in the brand. Amana knew it needed to make changes and make them quickly if it was to avoid closing factories. A targeted approach to reviving the brand was the only option.

An Accurate Diagnosis

The first step was to observe interactions of consumers in a retail setting with the different washers and dryers. It was soon apparent that there wasn't much to distinguish one brand from the other. It was the era of low-cost manufacturing, and the challenge seemed fairly straightforward: Stand out in a "sea of white" showroom.

Laundry is about cleaning and renewal, but the dull paint finish didn't communicate that. The control panels were devoid of color, reinforcing the idea that laundry was a chore. Aside from the convenience of having a washer and dryer in the home, the machines themselves offered little in terms of experience over going to the Laundromat.

RKS Design didn't have the time—or the mandate—to redesign everything. Ironically, quality, the trait Amana prided itself on, was not communicated to the consumer. There was nothing about the washers that called attention to valuable details such as the stainless steel tub. These features mattered only if consumers could be motivated to actually open the machine. How could an "Intel-inside" type of message be created in this segment?

Given the urgency of the design effort, RKS designers focused on attraction and engagement. Observation had shown that, when consumers did stop to interact in the showroom, they played around with the dials and studied the control panels. Because these areas attracted consumers, three immediate priorities were chosen for the design effort: badging, knobs, and graphics.

- **Badging**—A small badge that said "stainless" was introduced to communicate the added value of the stainless steel tub. The Amana name badge was also redone in a stainless steel finish to further underscore this long-lasting feature.

- **Knobs**—Soft-touch knobs were added to make the controls inviting and more user-friendly.
- **Graphics**—In a big departure from the rest of the industry, the design team focused on creating easily understood graphics using bright colors for the control panel.

Though RKS Design felt confident that this was the right approach, the proposed changes added an estimated $0.30 to the cost of goods sold and would not add functionality. It would be difficult to convince Amana's engineers, marketers, and executives to make the investment. It would be pointless to merely "tell" the other stakeholders how to proceed. It was critical to *show* them that the new approach would be effective in the marketplace. As Tom Matano, creator of the Mazda Miata observed, "The ultimate is to have a combination of aesthetics and experience, what I like to call empathic design. But aesthetics is important in calling attention to what is important about the design. If you're in the newspaper business and people keep missing the headline, there's a problem. Design has to act as the on/off switch; a signal about where you are."[5] Here, the validation had to come from the consumer.

A New Focus on Consumer Testing

Typical focus group testing—where consumers are brought in, shown a design concept, and asked to give feedback—would not be enough to turn the tide. This kind of consumer testing gives consumers an experience of being a "research subject" and is a poor predictor of actual market performance. To be relevant, the team knew they needed to give them a "buying experience." A fully developed design model was placed next to competitive products and the team watched to see how the consumers would react.

When the consumers came in, they were quickly attracted to the design changes. The color graphics made the products stand out in

the "sea of white" and the soft-touch knobs created immediate consumer engagement with the design, far more than observed with
competitive products (see Figure 2.2).

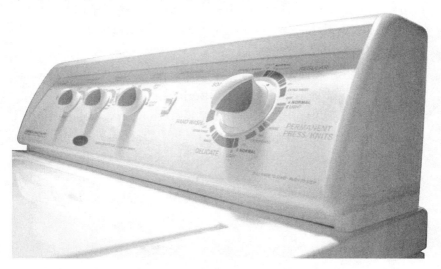

© RKS Design

Figure 2.2   Redesigned Amana laundry console

Seeing the enthusiastic response to the new design, Amana
agreed to proceed with it. In the end, that $0.30 increase in the cost
of goods increased perceived value significantly and translated into a
price increase of over $100 at retail. Retailers who had dropped the
brand began to sign on again. Amana realized more than $20 million
in annual profits from the new designs and embraced efforts to
redesign other categories.

Payoff also came in terms of feedback from the market. Changing
the graphics on the washer and dryer from gray to color not only
engaged consumers at retail, but mothers also reported that the color-
coded dials made it easier for them to teach their children how to do
laundry. The brand equity generated by the emotional connection
created by empowering women to teach their children cannot be
overstated.

Building Confidence, Building Success

Upon seeing measurable results, the team developed confidence in the methodology and themselves. Buoyed by success, the framework streamlined the design process as efforts began to revamp other segments in the Amana product line.

The next order of business was to re-create Amana's refrigerator and other major appliances lines. Both the design and corporate teams were eager to build emotional connections based on consumer insight. One line of refrigerators featured a "Kid Zone" on the inside of the refrigerator door (see Figure 2.3). Located on the bottom third of the door, this playful, engaging zone allowed mothers to store their children's snacks and drinks at a height within easy reach for them.

© RKS Design

Figure 2.3   Amana refrigerator with Kid Zone (penguin)

Playing on the fact that the kitchen was often the "heart of the home," some fridges included a voice recorder that enabled families to leave messages for one another, rather than writing notes—an early iteration of the "intelligent appliance."

The results of the redesigns succeeded in the marketplace far beyond anyone's expectations. Amana recovered from being invisible in consumer ratings to being ranked second out of seven brands considered. More important, people were interested in the company again. As John Herrington put it, "There was a huge impact inside the company as a result of this process. The whole organization was energized...people enjoyed making cool products instead of just struggling. And we were able to attract more talent as a result...."[6]

What made the designers the happiest? When asked the highlight of this project for them, the response was unanimous: "We saved jobs by keeping the plant running." It was clear that the executives and designers did more than empathize with each other's challenges. They made those challenges their own. Emotional connections are not for consumers alone.

Eventually, Amana was acquired by Maytag following its brand revival, and the signature badge was later imitated by other brands. However, the success of the design process was not simply a matter of the right sketches and embellishments. It involved as much change inside the company as in the appliances. Finding the right touch points allowed the company to reconnect with its core consumers. It also allowed the time, freedom, and financial standing to create and execute bolder concepts that built on the momentum from the laundry segment.

Moving Forward

The stories of companies competing—and *winning*—by using design are increasing in number. We see that the state of design is undergoing the kind of transformation that the IT revolution brought a decade ago. Then, there was a period of intense experimentation and rush to install "the latest and greatest." Many of these concepts faded into obscurity when they didn't respond to any real needs and desires of consumers. Today, the platforms that people have adopted—Facebook, LinkedIn, Google—have become part of the lives of those who use them. People trust, share, and evangelize these platforms.

These changes weren't just because of better tools. Inside companies, too, managers learned how to ask the right questions, guide the implementation process, and make choices that fit with their strategies and brand promises. We believe that the same dynamic is possible with great design. Tom Matano goes further, saying, "In medieval times, the arts flourished because kings were patrons of the arts. In today's world, managers can be patrons of design.... They must understand that the product is ultimately the billboard of their corporate strategy."[7]

Psycho-Aesthetics helps to create that bridge between design and strategy. It fosters communication between individuals and departments and, ultimately, with the consumer. By giving everyone a common, visual, quantifiable vocabulary that has a basis in both logic *and* emotion, teams are empowered to make meaningful emotional connections with consumers.

Creating Meaning

Design changes, even aesthetic ones, have the power to profoundly change and shape the consumer experience. Understanding the implications of various alternatives in emotional terms enables stakeholders to make decisions that support the interests of the firm and consumers. Too often, difficult trade-offs are made based on financial metrics because they seem more concrete. However, basic emotional responses apply to all consumer behaviors, and these responses can and should be analyzed objectively. Establishing an emotional context to harness the implicit knowledge of teams not only creates a common language, but it also creates a stage for meaningful dialogue—and design—to happen.

3

Map the Future

Design is a process that begins with a deep understanding of the consumer. Consumer experience experts Lewis Carbone and Steve Haeckel wrote, "Customers always get more than they bargained for, because a product or service always comes with an experience. By experience we mean the take-away impression formed by people's encounters with products, services, and businesses...."[1] *Great design begins with understanding the industry and competitive offerings according to consumer experience and empowerment.*

But how can you evaluate subjective and intangible ideas such as experience and empowerment? Traditional tools for mapping the competition generally rely on analyzing pricing, margins, and market shares. Although these metrics will always be important, they don't begin to capture the importance of the emotional connection that distinguishes market leaders in every category. Furthermore, financial measures give us a snapshot of today. To establish a direction for future innovation, the competitive landscape must be understood in the context of consumers. The key to developing truly breakthrough products and services can be found in first *understanding* the consumer experience and then innovating meaningful ways of *transforming* it. The very best innovations transform both the experience and the consumer.

Consider the runaway success of the Flip Video camcorder, which upon introduction quickly commanded 13 percent of the camcorder market *despite the fact that 50 percent of its users already owned a camcorder*. For the two years prior to the Flip cam's release, the camcorder category was stagnant. The outlook was grim with widespread expectations for decline. But the executives at Pure Digital Technologies, at the time an unknown player, saw things differently. They saw opportunity, so they boldly entered the market with a camcorder that had the point-and-click functionality of a Polaroid camera. The Flip cam's small size made it easy to take anywhere, eliminating the need to tote around a camera bag. The picture quality was far superior to the other portable camcorder substitute—the cell phone—and the Flip cam performed above expectations in dimly lit environments. Best of all, its preloaded software and USB connector that "flipped" out at the press of a button made uploading videos to YouTube effortless. Soon after its release, the Flip cam became Amazon.com's top-selling camcorder, and it surpassed sales expectations at major retailers. Bloggers began telling stories about their children and elderly relatives making and sharing video recordings minutes after taking the Flip cam out of the box.

This unbridled success was not the result of projecting the future of the camcorder technology. It was the result of a deep thought process about how to deliver a better consumer experience. Before the Flip cam, the essence of the consumer camcorder experience was confusing and difficult. Technophobes who could barely transfer pictures from their still digital cameras steered clear of the capable but complicated offerings on the camcorder aisle.

By recognizing this major untapped market, Pure Digital had the insight to bring fun and ease of use into the camcorder experience. They understood that people didn't want to become videographers. They merely wanted to share the moments of their lives with the people they loved. By eliminating a few major pain points (challenges faced by consumers as they interact with a design) through stripping away unnecessary features and adding built-in USB and an automated uploading system, Flip became an extremely attractive option for a wide variety of users, finding its own niche in the "whitespace" between cell phones, digital cameras, and existing camcorders. The stripped-down design of the Flip cam also allowed a price point of approximately $200—well within the reach of the college students and other new consumers Pure Digital was seeking to connect with.

The decisions about what features to include or leave out were not guided by a desire to outpace competitors. The consumer experience was the focus of Flip Video's executive team as it sought to redefine the market. Though the camera was designed by Smart Design (with investment from IDEO), the mission of Pure Digital was clear. Simon Fleming-Wood, Vice President of marketing for Pure Digital Technologies, explains:

> "When we started out, we had simplicity as our goal. There are two ways to go about simplicity—by making something stupid, or by making its benefits accessible. We initially tried to do a one-time-use camcorder, but there were business model challenges with that concept. But most of our consumers were women, and, in the traditional camcorder market, most of the buyers were hobbyists and dads.... We learned that moms were a big category that was left out.

> "The camcorder market was stagnant when we began, but we saw that it was only about 1/6th the size of the still camera market. In fact, in 2000, we saw that the camcorder market was where the still camera market was 25–30 years prior. We were confident that there was great potential if the overall experience could be simplified to a point-and-click functionality.

> "We knew that people really liked video, but we knew that the experience needed to be changed and that there was tremendous value in doing so. We also understood before the

design process even began that the product was the marketing...it had to be the thing that everyone talked about. In the end, we were able to create a beautiful device that is not intimidating to anyone.

"We were initially labeled 'camcorder lite,' but today there are pictures of Steven Spielberg and Steven Soderebergh using their Flip cams—and they certainly have knowledge and access to the best equipment. I think the simplicity that we built into the camera made it fun for the tech-savvy as well. Our success was really about re-imagining the future. It is really gratifying to see new products enter the market and refer to themselves as 'the Flip of their category....' Many of our competitors had all the capabilities we had, but they could not put the same package together."[2]

Although the insight to begin with consumer experience makes sense when it is explained, it represents a major departure from the strategy development process in many organizations. When you've determined the desired consumer experience, this vision must be the focus of execution at every turn from strategy, design, and engineering to marketing. Notice, in discussing the Flip cam, there was no mention of pixels, memory, or other technical specifications. The strategy was pared down to three essentials: a) affordability for new consumer segments, b) ease of use, and c) ease of sharing content. There was no software to download or install to share content, no cords to tangle or lose. The Flip was battery-powered, so if you ran out of power on vacation, you weren't out of luck because of a forgotten charger. You could just buy spare batteries at the nearest store. Best of all, the Flip was actually fun to use. It forever shortened the distance between capturing a memory and sharing it. The payoff of the consumer-centric design was obvious—sales reached almost two million units in less than two years.[3]

The camcorder industry quickly awoke to the idea that the relevant market for camcorders had suddenly expanded from the traditional techie hobbyists and dads to anyone who wanted and needed to record memories. At the same time as Flip gained market share, the industry was growing as well, due to the introduction of similar offerings from competitors.

Although existing consumers do look for new features in categories such as camcorders, the rules were rewritten, and the market expanded by creating a design that was simple and accessible. These designs infused the market with excitement and hordes of Flip cam evangelists eager to share their memories *and* their discovery of a better way to shoot and share video (see Figure 3.1).

© RKS Design

Figure 3.1　The Flip camcorder

Designing for Tomorrow's Markets Today

Short of hiring a soothsayer, how can you predict what experience consumers want? Depending on your industry, development cycles may be anywhere from a few months to several years. It's hard enough to predict what technical specifications will be possible in the near future, surely something as complex as "experience" must be even more challenging to anticipate. Looking at sales figures and internal cost structures forces the discussion into the present, not the future. Mapping margins and market share is no more effective. Though executives and stockholders may connect emotionally with market share, consumers do not. Statistics-based approaches also skew resources toward known revenue-generators at the expense of discovering where breakout innovations and future profits may reside. Teams working from strategy borne of market share examination can become focused on demonstrating compliance rather than vision. The products and services work, but they may no longer work for the consumer. When this happens, the ability to create new categories with staying power diminishes rapidly.

Experience Mapping Guides the Way

If margins and market shares aren't the full answer, how then can a company translate the trends and data into products, services, and experiences that consumers actually want? How can data be gathered when standards are still emerging? And how can design focused on experience be leveraged to create business results?

These were the questions that sparked a long process of discovery and experimentation. The business battlefield is littered with failures—attractive products that failed to connect with their audience. Although a variety of tools are available to measure consumers' response to products and services *after* they've been created, development teams need to predict how to connect emotionally with diverse groups of consumers *before* beginning the development process.

With examination of notable successes and failures, we turned our attention to understanding the complex human emotions attached to the purchase and post-purchase experiences. New tools were developed to capture our lessons. For example, in doing research for Amana, we found that the competitive drive to show off to the neighbors co-existed with a deep desire to nurture family and

Freedom to Innovate

Frank Tyneski, former executive director of the Industrial Designers Society of America and a prolific designer for Motorola and Research in Motion (RIM) Blackberry, credits his success to the fact that he began his career as a toy designer at Fisher Price. He notes that the proposals for new toys were often less than a page and allowed teams to have fun and experiment with new ideas. On the other hand, the requests for proposals (RFPs) for new phones often resembled the phone book. Focus on consumer experience becomes even *more* important as technology becomes more complex. In such cases, it's more critical than ever that the requirements should be framed broadly enough that novel solutions can be explored. After all, an RFP to improve the typewriter would never have given birth to the PC.

Although understanding technical details is important in many industries—including toys—creating a story around the consumer experience makes the effort more concrete and meaningful to teams. Innovation efforts work better when people understand what they will *enable people to do*, rather than just working toward a price point or feature set. Getting to one page may not always be possible, but the principle of simplicity matters.

friends. We quickly realized that we couldn't talk about emotion without developing a common understanding among our clients and ourselves. For consumer insights to guide the design process, we had to be specific about what was relevant and within our power to influence. We also had to develop the tools in a way that they would connect with our audience at hand—the stakeholders within our clients' companies.

We worked with anthropologists and academics to formalize the intuitive process our design teams had been using for years. Our goal was to develop a methodology that could help us create a predictable process for identifying strategic opportunities to create breakthrough consumer experiences. What was needed was a way to visualize the marketplace in the context of consumer emotions and experience. To do this, we created Psycho-Aesthetics® mapping.

Mapping Emotions

Psycho-Aesthetics maps are X–Y grids where the vertical axis represents emotion and the horizontal axis represents interactivity. *Emotion and interactivity combine to form experience.* To quantify emotion, we looked to the foundational psychological theory expressed in Maslow's Hierarchy of Needs. This hierarchy illustrates how human needs and emotions are prioritized. Physiological needs are the needs for the most basic things required to survive—food, water, shelter, and so on. These survival needs must be met before we seek to satisfy our needs for security. As each level of needs is met, we can move up the pyramid, gradually moving through the needs for love and esteem until reaching self-actualization, the pinnacle of human development, in which we have become the best possible version of ourselves.

Psycho-Aesthetics translates Maslow's Hierarchy of Needs into a Consumer's Hierarchy of Needs, Desires, and Aspirations, as shown in Figure 3.2. In the Consumer's Hierarchy, the first level represents the products and experiences that satisfy the most basic needs in a category. These get the job done, but they don't significantly transform a consumer's life or their outlook on life.

A study of our own history and that of iconic brands revealed that the biggest successes had one thing in common: The products and experiences that people bonded with were the ones that *made them feel good about themselves*. Nike shoes make people feel like better athletes. Organic produce makes people feel like better providers. Luxury cars make people feel successful. These are the things that do more than simply get the job done. They enable people to become

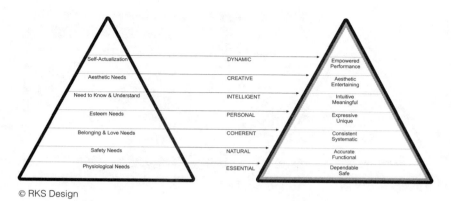

© RKS Design

Figure 3.2   Transformation of Maslow's Hierarchy of Needs (left) to Consumer's Hierarchy of Needs, Desires, and Aspirations (right)

more. Think of what a global positioning system (GPS) does for a nervous driver or the perfect suit does for the nervous job seeker. Products and experiences that satisfy higher-level needs help people become more evolved versions of themselves.

In the Consumer's Hierarchy, Dynamic Empowerment is the pinnacle of consumer desires, needs, and aspirations. The most meaningful consumer experiences provide this high level of empowerment. By empowerment, we mean the emotional connections we make with products and services because they help us to do things we couldn't do (or couldn't do as well) without them. They may do this by giving us more time (a dishwasher), by allowing us to connect (Skype, Facebook), or by adding fun to our lives (Wii). There are products and services in every category that empower us to different degrees, and they often change the way we interact with the world around us.

When consumers feel empowered, they develop a profound emotional bond with the products that enabled this transformation (see Figure 3.3). This leads to brand loyalty and evangelism, offering an opportunity to radically change not only consumer lives, but also the direction of firms and entire industries.

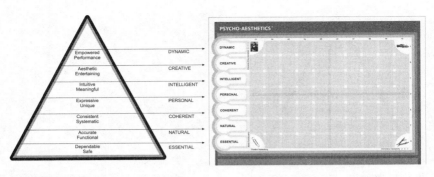

© RKS Design

Figure 3.3   Maslow's Hierarchy and the Psycho-Aesthetics Map. The Hierarchy corresponds to the vertical (Y) axis.

Engaging Interactivity

Interactivity is the second dimension of consumer experience represented on Psycho-Aesthetics maps. The horizontal (or X) axis is based on the design's level of interactivity...from passive interactivity to highly immersive. Although function can be a part of a design's level of interactivity, this axis also serves to measure how many senses are activated and how deeply engaging the overall interactivity is.

Interactivity also considers the way in which people come to adopt—or dismiss the things they encounter in their daily lives. We use the degree to which a consumer is compelled to interact (play, examine, test-drive) with an offering to judge this. Interactivity can be observed reliably and is highly correlated with interest and purchase behaviors. Companies succeed when they engage as many senses as possible. People who touch products are more likely to buy them. Grocery store receipts increase when music is played. And who hasn't fallen prey to the allure of that "new car smell"?

Interactivity can be seen and measured. One of the most successful illustrations of this idea was our work on Teddy Ruxpin, the toy industry's first computer-animated, talking stuffed bear. It is still one of the best selling toys of all time. Children have always engaged in play-acting and many toys at the time were offering more sensory feedback (such as Strawberry Shortcake, which had a particular scent) and more accessories, varieties, and features (for example, the Barbie and GI Joe franchises). Teddy Ruxpin actually spoke back to children and interacted with them. This wasn't just a toy; this was *their friend*. The technology inside of Teddy and the mechanisms required to change the audio tapes had to be carefully crafted to make sure that the illusion was not destroyed. Rather than engaging in passive play, which can quickly become boring, children played with Teddy Ruxpin for longer periods of time, became more attached, and created elaborate adventures involving the bear. This increased level of involvement with the brand created a success that continues to the present day: Since its inception in 1985, more than 20 million units of Teddy Ruxpin toys and merchandise have been sold worldwide. Brand recognition remains at a high 80 percent.[4]

As illustrated by Teddy Ruxpin, the amount of interaction that is encouraged by the design is a critical test of its success. Although there are devices such as the garage door opener that need to work at the touch of the button and then fade quickly into the background, these products rarely generate that consumer fervor that leads to explosive growth. More deeply engaging experiences move people and can turn them quickly into brand evangelists. Listening to a music CD is, for the most part, a passive act. The iTunes/iPod experience allows consumers to easily and immediately download a song to their iPod so that it can be enjoyed as part of an exercise routine or commute engages the consumer as it elevates the experience. Now look at Guitar Hero. By enabling the consumer to become an active participant in the music, the gaming franchise was propelled past the $1 billion mark in North America in a record 26 months. The choice to participate rather than be a passive bystander is a powerful lure at any age.

Mapping Out the Possibilities

This mapping enables powerful analyses of personas, competitive products, brands and more, all as seen through the lens of consumer experience. Items placed on these maps fall into one of four quadrants: Basic, Versatile, Artistic, and Enriched, as shown in Figure 3.4.

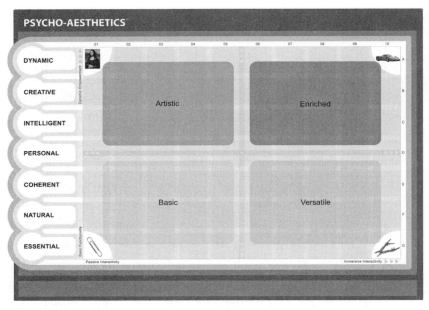

© RKS Design

Figure 3.4   Psycho-Aesthetics map with quadrants named

- **Basic quadrant**—In the lower-left quadrant of the Psycho-Aesthetics map is a paper clip. This represents a product that is purely functional and requires little involvement from the user. The lower-left quadrant would include very basic items that have limited purposes (for example, a bare-bones can opener).
- **Versatile quadrant**—On the lower-right quadrant, a multi-tool offers high levels of functionality and invites interaction from the user. Complex technology and multiuse devices dominate this quadrant.
- **Artistic quadrant**—On the upper-left quadrant is the Mona Lisa, which represents pure beauty but does not provide much

function or interaction. Items in this category include high-end fashion and jewelry.

- **Enriched quadrant**—Represented in the upper-right corner by the Ferrari, items in this quadrant combine function and beauty. They engage multiple senses—visual, tactile (leather, controls), auditory (the distinctive purr of the engine). These purchases are driven by higher-level emotional needs and motivated by the consumer's desire for self-expression. Our choices in homes and cars are good examples of lifestyle and recreation purchases that result in immersive and empowering experiences.

Although the Mona Lisa and Ferrari represent high levels of beauty and high levels of interactivity and empowerment, respectively, they do not necessarily translate into high price points. This mapping tool is as relevant for entry-level products as it is for high-end ones. The idea of using products to represent the corners of the map is to provide a reference point for experience that everyone in the team can relate to. The goal is to understand the specific experiences that will be valuable to target consumers—whatever the segment may be.

One caveat is that *the number of interactions does not equate to the quality of consumer experience.* A positive experience depends on the degree to which people can control their interactions and get feedback that they want. Anyone scrolling through Amazon.com can determine the level of detail in which they want to research a particular item. However, ordering is not the place where consumers want to navigate multiple screens—and Amazon knows that. One-click ordering is an equally important part of the equation. Understanding where effort will help you bond with consumers and where it will repel them is at the heart of good design. The experience of actually using a product or service needs to be considered along with the experiences that they enable.

A map of the cell phone industry can help to illustrate the concept of mapping products, as shown in Figure 3.5.

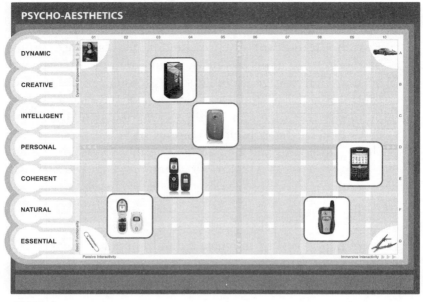

© RKS Design

Figure 3.5 Psycho-Aesthetics map showing competitive landscape for cell phones

If we look at the map of cell phones, the Basic quadrant includes phones for those who are interested primarily in calling. They may seek out a cell phone to take with them in emergencies or maintain contact with family members. They need something simple and easy to use.

The Artistic quadrant includes the phones that have a high degree of personal style. The aesthetics of the phone are distinctive and the primary basis of attraction for this consumer. Some of these consumers may also be seeking out kits and accessories to decorate and beautify other phones—or limited edition colors and designs to show self-expression.

In the Versatile quadrant are phones that have multiple functions such as email access, data feeds, or a camera. People in this quadrant likely depend on their phone for professional and personal use and are looking for reliability.

The Enriched quadrant would require creating a phone that combines multiple functions with style and engaging features that can be used for fun and entertainment as well as for work. This is a new area of competition today.

Strategy Based on Understanding

We can begin to understand how an industry is evolving by placing competitive products or services on the map. Which companies just get the job done (paper clip)? Who offers beautiful objects that don't necessarily engage you in a rich multisensory experience (Mona Lisa)? Which items offer interaction but don't necessarily create rich, empowering experience? Where are the examples in your industry of the Ferrari—a combination of beauty and immersive interactivity? The placement of various offerings on the map is a qualitative assessment, but it can quickly and efficiently establish direction by highlighting the gaps in current offerings in terms of the consumer experience.

Team collaboration in this stage is highly encouraged. Inclusion of all departmental functions playing a role in implementation will develop the consensus and vision required to create meaningful innovation. Because the information is represented visually, it can be easily recorded and referenced throughout the design process. And going back to visual reference points of your strategy is a critical part of helping teams to keep the product development process focused on the vision of creating a better consumer experience.

Experience Mapping and the Power of Design

If we look back at the Flip camcorder example, we can see how the power of design can shift a product or service from one quadrant to another. Before the Flip cam, the competitive landscape for camcorders was largely clustered in the "versatile" quadrant as both existing consumers and products were focused on technology and features. The executives at Pure Digital realized there was a massive, untapped, market segment in the upper-left quadrant. By reducing complexity and adding fun and style, the Flip cam appealed to these consumers who were driven by the emotional need to connect and share their memories with loved ones but lacked an affinity for the highly technical.

The Value of Experience-Based Mapping

Focus on benefits, not features. The mapping of offerings on the basis of consumer experience keeps teams focused on the benefits and values the experience delivers and helps avoid the temptation to focus solely on the features. Features alone do not create emotional connection...it's only when the consumer experience creates real benefits that the bond between consumers and brand is formed.

Establish clear priorities. Teams can understand the design elements that connect with consumers and focus their attention on amplifying or developing those. Even if money is no object, a strong design generally calls attention to only a few ideas to reach the consumer. Adding embellishments increases the chances of dissonance in many cases—and especially in very crowded categories.

Eliminate waste of resources. Teams can understand what can be safely pared away—even if it was valued at one time. This allows resources to be deployed to create an offering that is compelling to new and evolving consumers.

Pure Digital's success came out of its instinctive application of these principles. But even if you're blessed with a flash of insight, without a robust innovation and design process, the odds are stacked against repeated success. Furthermore, corporations rarely make decisions based on instinct. A rational basis for understanding and analysis is required for stakeholder and investor buy-in. And this is *exactly* what Psycho-Aesthetics provides. In the next few chapters, you learn how to use the suite of tools to methodically and repeatably uncover the emerging opportunities in your industry.

Connecting the Dots with Design

Design is an increasingly bigger part of strategy. Aside from helping concepts to stand out, there are three major reasons why design will continue to grow in importance:

Design and Corporate Performance

The link between design and corporate performance is becoming evident across industries. Why has Apple seen so much success with the iPod and iPhone? Design leadership. Poor design and customer service are also widely blamed when companies struggle. These are not just the opinions of analysts and experts, these sentiments are echoed by consumers. Design is becoming a proxy for the ability of companies to execute and monetize their strategies. Whether you want to get to the top or stay there, you need to pay attention to design.

Convergence of Brand and Design

The idea of what was considered "brand" is rapidly converging with what was traditionally "design." Nike, Target, and Google are some of the darlings of the brand world. But they are also held up as examples of great design. It is becoming increasingly difficult to separate branding from design. The promise of a hybrid car cannot come with the body of a Hummer. Even outside of consumer categories, innovations must have their benefits communicated through their designs.

The Need for Sustainability

The emerging concern with sustainability is forcing everyone—even those with strong designs—to revamp and pay close attention to issues such as use of materials and the handling of waste. This movement will force the redesign of innumerable products and services. Design can be used not only to create better products and services, but also to drive adoption of these concepts as well.

Design methodology can help ask the questions as it helps deliver solutions.

4

Personify Your Consumer

The next step in crafting an effective design strategy is developing a deep understanding of potential customers, what they seek in the category, and their needs, desires, and aspirations. Creating meaningful consumer experiences depends on these insights. Developing and mapping personas can enable companies to identify target consumers and set design priorities.

Redesigning an Icon

Leading audio products company JBL (James B. Lansing) Professional had a problem. After more than a decade as the leader in the portable powered speaker market it created with the original EON line of portable public address (PA) speakers, JBL's competition had begun encroaching on the EON's market share. In the years since its introduction in 1995, the EON had become a global product and sold nearly one million units...drawing more than 300 competitors into the category in the process. Though there was no single competitive threat, there were many "me too" products nipping at JBL's heels. The category was becoming commoditized. JBL knew it needed to take preemptive measures to retain market leadership. What it needed was a new generation of EON that raised the bar in all categories.

JBL set about creating just such a product. When its engineers felt they'd perfected the advanced technology required to offer a higher performance product at a substantially lower weight, it was natural to enlist an industrial design firm to create the new generation of EON...after all, the original EON was a product conceived in an industrial design (ID) firm.

Simon Jones, director of marketing for JBL Professional, summed up the challenge succinctly, "The bits that we do best are components and engineering. We make our own components— woofers, compression drives, tweeters, etc. and we can control those—and those are our competitive advantage. These are the bits you don't want to blow up. But we stick all of those things in a box. You don't see them at all. You can hear them but you don't see them. That was the challenge for us with design...to bring that same level of quality to the *outside*..."[1]

JBL's internal research showed that consumers relied heavily on visual cues to judge the quality of the speakers, even after every other factor was controlled. Retailers and company executives were aware that the speakers had to look good to sell, but the extent of the relationship between the visual appearance and audio judgments (even from professionals) was surprising. Producing and surpassing the sound quality that people had come to expect from JBL required significant investment in research and new technology. To command the required price at retail, the speakers and other products had to communicate the value of the superior technology inside with a clear and compelling design language.

JBL engaged our design team to analyze the market, consumers, and opportunities, and to then provide analyses and recommendations as to how best to use design to communicate the value of the new lower-weight technology to showcase the well-recognized JBL brand DNA and most of all, to connect with buyers. The starting point for creating such a strategy was developing a deep understanding of the consumer.

Personas—The Mask of the Consumer

In Latin, the term *persona* refers to an actor's mask...a tool once used to help an actor assume a character. In marketing and industrial design, a persona still represents a fictional character—but rather than used for assuming a role in a play, individual personas are created to represent user types and market segments.

The persona method has its roots in the software industry in which Alan Cooper[2] is widely credited with laying the foundations for using personas to guide the design process. Cooper came upon the use of personas naturally—intuitively imagining a single target user in his own software development process. Much like an actor in a play, Cooper would quite literally play act how users would accomplish their job as he created a user interface. It wasn't until Cooper moved from software designing to consulting that he suddenly realized the need and value of using personas to achieve clarity and understanding among development team members.

Personas aren't just dreamed up. They're constructed as the result of careful research. An individual persona is a fictional representation of real users. Though personas aren't real, it is vital that they *feel* real to all stakeholders. A basic persona can include a name, photo, age, income, and family status. It describes and illustrates their likes and dislikes; what's important to them; and their behavior traits, perspectives, skills, and goals. Most important, each persona includes specific insight into what they seek in the market category at hand and how they relate to a specific experience or product. Ultimately, a persona embodies the needs, desires, and aspirations of the users it represents.

Personas Fuel Intelligent, User-Centric Design

Today, personas are a valuable tool for guiding strategy, design, and innovation regardless of the industry. Personas transform data into the context of consumer experience. When used appropriately, personas help stakeholders make sense of volumes of data, empathize with consumers, and mitigate risks by clarifying goals.

- **Bringing data to life**—The motivations and thought processes of consumers are critical inputs that can determine the success of new concepts. But all too often these insights get buried in data. The sheer volume of data contributes to the confusion, but even more problematic is the lack of depth and meaningful context to the numbers. As a result, products and services tend to get compared to the competition based on features and price points. But what consumers want to know is *how the product or service fits into their lives*. This is also *exactly* what design teams *need* to know. Personas bring this invaluable context to life so that the needs, desires, and aspirations of target consumers can inform the development process.

- **Engaging the power of empathy**—Personas help teams develop an affinity for the people they are designing for. They find parallels with friends, family, and associates and draw inspiration from their traits. Empathizing with the needs and aspirations of individuals creates focus, understanding, and excitement for all stakeholders in the design process. We all know what we would never buy and why; personas help a team develop this understanding for a variety of users. Personas don't just put a face on an otherwise abstract user—although that is valuable. Indeed, much like the actor's mask, deftly drawn personas allow designers to see the world and the design through the eyes of a specific type of user. This vision suddenly makes it clear what matters...what needs are prioritized for this user, what visual and tactile cues will attract them, what features have relevance, and which are superfluous.

Many of the greatest stories of innovation are actually stories of empathy. The idea for creating OXO Good Grips kitchen tools originated as Sam Farber watched his wife struggle to use a vegetable peeler with arthritic hands. The ability to see a developing design from another perspective makes them an important tool for all stakeholders.

- **Mitigating risk through clarity**—When data is brought to life in the context of personas, it's suddenly easier to find disconnects with the data or with company aims. Inauthentic personas—ones that are drawn from real data but don't resonate in real life—are easily spotted. Personas that are not immediately recognizable to brand executives can open up a dialog and lead to new insights.

Clearly defined personas also help teams avoid the pitfalls of either designing according to their own preferences or constructing an idea of the end user to fit the design, rather than designing for clearly targeted end users. The value of innovation is directly proportionate to the degree to which it connects with consumers. Steelcase CEO James Hackett famously challenges his managers presenting new ideas with the question, "What's the user insight that led to this product?"[3] The development of personas forces teams to demonstrate that they have digested and understood the data, which then enables them to set and agree to design priorities. This can prevent design failures such as creating a complicated kitchen gadget for a segment of users who have little time to devote to cooking.

The magic of presenting carefully drawn personas to an interdisciplinary team comes in the murmurs of instant recognition, "Hey, I know that guy!" This recognition can often bring valuable refinement as team members add insights that can be synthesized into the personas. Everyone has a clear idea of who a persona is and isn't. "Bob wouldn't do that." Or "That would appeal to Terri, but Jill would hate it." This clear consensus inspires teams and helps stakeholders stay on track through long and complex development cycles. Teams focused on designing for the target users bring the most return on investment. Personas deliver this focus.

What Goes into a Persona

Although the depth of personas can be scaled on a project-by-project basis, the richer the persona, the more value it brings to the design process. The most common data sources for developing personas are ethnography, demographics, market research, and consumer analytics (see Figure 4.1).

- **Demographics**—Companies have an obvious need to know the general size of the target populations and purchasing power of their consumers through the use of demographic information. Demographics are especially helpful in ensuring segments are not overlooked and that segment sizes are considered when projecting potential return on investment (ROI).

- **Market research**—In established categories, consumer feedback about products and services can be useful, especially for identifying remaining pain points or suggestions for improvement. This research can be conducted through surveys, interviews, or by "listening in" as consumers talk online about their experiences in reviews, blog posts, forums, and tweets.

- **Consumer analytics**—Companies such as Amazon and Netflix have demonstrated the value of sophisticated consumer analytics. You know, those "if you like A, you might also like B" suggestions? That's consumer analytics in action. Costco chief Jim Sinegal, for example, knows that toilet paper and bananas are items that appear in many shoppers' baskets, so he prioritizes keeping their prices low.[4]

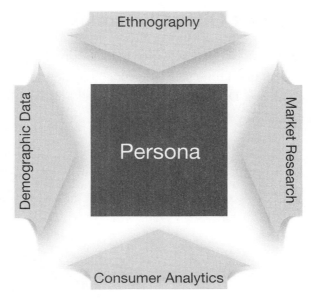

© RKS Design

Figure 4.1   Inputs for persona development

- **Ethnography**—Ethnography is simply a detailed observation of human behavior. It is an elevated form of people-watching that includes notes on times spent on various stages of an activity and consumer reactions to their environment. Companies also use tools such as eyeball tracking and mystery shoppers to capture data that might otherwise be lost (for example, perhaps a consumer ultimately purchased Special K but spent 5 minutes looking at Cocoa Puffs). Shadowing consumers through the purchase process provided invaluable insight in the Amana case in Chapter 2, "Enable Your Stakeholders."

What You Get Out of Personas

Although the depth and scope of persona development can be scaled dependent upon timelines and scope, fully developed personas incorporate Persona Dashboards, Day (or Week)-in-the-Life scenarios, Triggers, and Key Attractors (see Figure 4.2).

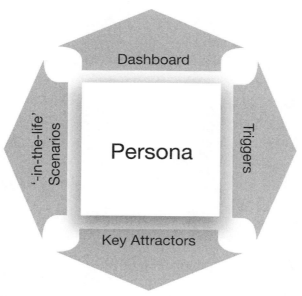

© RKS Design

Figure 4.2   Outputs from persona development

- **Persona Dashboard**—A persona dashboard gives a comprehensive snapshot of the user types in question. Beyond a name and photo, the dashboard includes key demographic information (for example, age, gender, income, family, location, and so on) and a narrative about who they are and, in particular, how they approach products and designs in the category under consideration. Often, dashboards also include information that gives insight to the personas' taste—what they wear, how they spend free time, what other products they buy, and what brands they use.

- **Triggers**—Triggers are the intangible things a product delivers. For example, some want control above all else. Others need ease-of-use. Still others are driven by desires to nurture others. Triggers run a spectrum from strictly rational to completely emotional. Identifying and prioritizing which triggers are most important to specific personas is an essential step in understanding how users will relate to market offerings.

- **"-in-the-Life" scenarios**—Day- and Week-in-the-Life scenarios dive deeper into a typical day or week of the personas. What activities fill their days? What challenges arise? Understanding the constraints and usage scenarios that are likely to take place creates an intimacy with the consumers and helps identify pleasure and pain points (aspects of a process that are either fun or the source of challenges and discomfort) in the consumer experience. These can effectively inform the design process, guiding teams to better understand which solutions will connect best with consumers.

- **Key Attractors**—Although triggers are intangibles, key attractors are much more concrete. These are the specific design features that engage a particular target group of consumers. For example, a new mother may be attracted to baby products whose features can be operated with one hand. These Key Attractors can also be evaluated against existing market offerings (see Figure 4.3).

Persona development generates insights that would have otherwise been forever trapped within piles of consumer research. Constructing fully developed personas is a time-consuming yet invaluable process. Empowering design teams to see the marketplace through personas enables them to understand and draw inspiration from consumer experience.

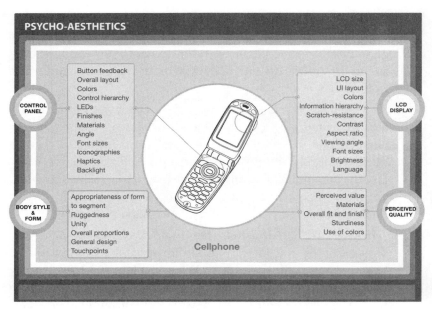

© RKS Design

Figure 4.3   Key attractors for cell phone concepts

Using Personas to Guide Design

When JBL approached us to redesign its iconic line of EON speakers, we quickly realized that the purchasers of powered portable speakers encompassed an incredibly diverse array of individuals and institutions. The team began by speaking with musicians, rental houses, retailers, and all other kinds of users, from churches to corporate settings. We also worked directly with several dozen department managers of Guitar Center, all of whom were musicians and users of the product, to gain further insight and feedback on our design directions.

The single most critical finding was that *people use EONs to make their living*. The speaker was a professional tool for many, and the addressable market was expanding to include "prosumers." The people who fell into this category included those who pursued music/DJ activities on the side and needed a reliable and powerful system.

Next, the team studied consumer reviews to learn what features consumers loved and hated about existing products. Detailed Persona Dashboards and Day-in-the-Life scenarios were created to develop a better understanding of how the wide variety of EON consumers interacted with their speakers.

The usage scenarios that were described during interviews were acted out by members of the design team using a wide range of products in the category. In the course of our research, we heard from musicians who piled all their gear in a van or pickup in the morning, drove four hours, set up, performed two shows, and then had to break down and reload their equipment for their late night return home. For rental houses, having equipment available that looked powerful and remained in good condition over time was important. As more people came into the market, it was important that the setup become as painless as possible. The benefit of the lighter-weight technology soon became apparent as the team struggled with offerings that were bulky, heavy, and difficult to mount.

A narrative was also developed for each major category of consumers. Although everyone spoke about the need for great sound, this was not a revelation. It was also the area in which JBL engineers had the greatest credibility. The importance of styling was also becoming an issue as more competitors entered the market. Retailers had expressed a desire for a high-quality "look" but were vague about what that entailed. The speaker had to communicate power and durability but also draw attention to the new lightweight technology. These disparate goals required a design that could capture a wide range of needs—image, reliability, and better user experience.

Mapping Personas

After personas have been developed, they can be mapped just like products were mapped in Chapter 3, "Map the Future." Although it may at first feel odd to put people on an X–Y grid, when you realize placement is framed by the consumer experience and based on a specific product or service category, such placement becomes clear. As with products, persona placement is based on the Consumer's Hierarchy of Needs, Desires, and Aspirations (vertical axis), as shown in Figure 3.3, and the relative interactivity of the experience (horizontal axis). You might expect, for example, to find a highly technical engineer persona placed somewhere in the lower-right Versatile quadrant, as shown in Figure 3.4. On the other hand, someone who is focused on high aesthetics and a simple user experience would be placed in the Artistic quadrant in the upper-left quadrant of the map.

It is important to remember that the same individual can take on different personas according to the category. For example, a woman may have emotional needs in the Artistic quadrant when looking for a handbag (for example, looking for something aesthetically distinctive) but may be in the Versatile quadrant when shopping for a car (for example, the primary focus may be on safety, reliability, and price). A successful bachelor may be an Enriched persona when looking for cars or clothes and a Basic consumer for kitchen implements. Although some of the personas may seem familiar, they should be reevaluated as new products are developed. Their lives evolve quickly, and a reality check often yields insights that can change the course of a design. It also gives the teams a chance to go into the design process with the current understanding of the consumer's life.

During the development process, personas are refreshed on a continual basis. The placement of personas on the map depends on how well the category is established. For existing offerings, preferences and pain points are known. In new categories, placements are qualitative judgments inferred by other choices in their lives such as cars, books, and music. This is a process that relies on the professional assessment and experience of designers and a careful selection of target consumers.

To go back to our example of the cell phone segment (see Figure 4.4), a persona map shows the needs of various individuals represented by a persona. These placements apply only to this category.

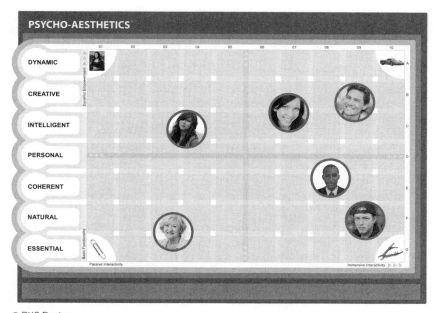

© RKS Design

Figure 4.4   Mapping of personas for the cell phone segment

In the **Basic quadrant** (lower left), Mary wants an easy-to-use cell phone to make calls when she is out with friends. She prefers to make longer calls from her home and does not talk on the cell phone while she's driving. It is important to her to know that she can reach her family in case of an emergency.

In the **Artistic quadrant** (upper left) is Kylie. She loves fashion and trends as a way to express herself. She uses the phone mainly for talking to friends and texting and wants something that looks unique and fits in with her style.

In the **Versatile quadrant** (lower right), Trent and Joseph have different professions but travel for their work and need to keep in touch with a wide network of people, review documents, call in to meetings, and manage their schedules. They need a reliable cell phone and service. They are interested in multiple functions and speed when they look for a device.

In the **Enriched quadrant** (upper right), Sabrina and Tim are looking for function as well as some fun and style. They have moderate phone use but use their computers for games, music, and connecting with friends. These activities take up a lot of their spare time. They would be interested in a phone that combines beauty with functions that can be used for both work and entertainment.

In the case of JBL, it was clear that, though the target personas demanded great sound, they also needed great portability—a desire few of them could articulate at the time. As we looked at interactions in the marketplace and in retail settings, we understood how consumers tested speaker weights. They knew they'd be lugging these things around for years to come. Reading a weight on a box meant little. Lifting a speaker and feeling the weight was what gave users a real sense of the product.

Persona analysis also made it clear that, despite the breakthrough technology JBL packed into the new EON, great sound was a baseline—a minimum requirement. The best opportunities for improving the consumer experience lay in *enhancing portability*. After developing a list of Key Attractors, we set about delivering JBL's high-performance technology in a design that was more functional and portable than ever before.

Getting a Handle on the Right Design

Even with stakeholders aligned on these goals, creating a design that addressed the needs of targeted users was a complex challenge. In a church or school, for example, the appearance of the speakers became part of the overall architecture because it was often elevated during events. For bands and DJs, the look of the speaker had to reinforce the music and image of the musicians. For all settings, the speakers needed to convey a sense of power and quality.

To do this, a distinctive "face" for the speaker was created. It included bold port vents to provide a visual accent and evoke fond memories of the original EON. A squat "bulldog" appearance was developed to indicate the ruggedness and workhorse performance. A perforated metal grille was added to protect the components and reinforce the impression of quality. These features needed to be balanced with the real-world usage scenarios that had been observed. To minimize abuse to the speaker and users alike, the design team removed all hard edges and corners. This made the EON durable and comfortable to move around. There are no corners to bash into knees and legs or to catch and gouge as they're slid in and out of cars. The new shape also helped to prevent the speakers getting banged up when corners get bumped in transit. Testing validated that the aesthetics were successful with consumers. The new design made people feel good about themselves by giving them confidence in the sound and appearance of their equipment. The uncluttered appearance also fit well in a variety of settings.

By understanding the challenges of consumers and rental companies transporting and stocking the equipment, all stakeholders understood that making it lighter was a huge benefit that could be leveraged. However, it was an attribute that consumers had to *discover* through interaction, because musicians and others in the category were primed to seek out the best sound quality. Thus, we included in our strategy a directive to create a design with a handle that begged consumers to pick it up. We knew that once they did, they would fall in love with JBL's new lighter-weight technology.

With this in mind, we gave the handles particular attention. This is where the speaker integrates with the user. First, our designers had to determine handle size, number, and placement—both to balance the weight and in consideration of how users would actually maneuver and carry this speaker. The EON features an on-board mini-mixer and puts out a massive 450 watts of power, yet weighs only 33 lbs—a full third less weight than competitors. To take full advantage the new light-weight technology, the flagship EON features three full-bar handles. Each handle, one on the top and one on each side, is placed for opti-mal ergonomics and balance and over-molded with a soft comfort-grip.

The top handle was also key to the retail experience (see Figure 4.5). After going to market, we observed the same response time and time again. The design invited people to pick up the speaker. They saw the EON sitting on the floor with the top handle calling out to them from a perfect mid-thigh height. After picking it up, consumers often did the same with competing products. Everything else suddenly felt heavy by comparison and *by design*. Inevitably, the consumer would return to the EON and smile. "Yeah, it really is that light."

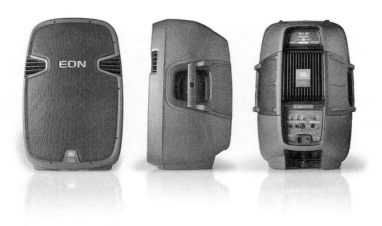

© RKS Design

Figure 4.5   JBL EON 515 speakers

The result of persona insight was a new EON that connected with consumers who knew that speakers need to "perform" even after the final song. And the EONs do exactly that. As one band leader for Judge Jackson praised, "Light as a feather. Good to use after a gig like that 'cause they're so friggin' light and accessible. That's what we want after exhausting ourselves on stage for the last three hours."[5] Users felt "heard" and understood. This was a speaker designed to fit their lives.

A Fresh Perspective

Adding a handle at the top of the speaker seems like an obvious choice today, but at the time it was not. Incorporating this feature required rebalancing internal components and was a topic of much debate with the executive and design teams. Because creating a superior design was a major part of this effort, a simple add-on wouldn't do. The proposed handle required a significant investment in molds and engineering to fit seamlessly with the design that had been created.

Well-executed innovations always *seem* obvious. The force of habit is so powerful that both companies and consumers often adjust to difficult situations rather than correcting them. Consider that despite the size of the home-improvement industry in the United States, it was only in 2002 that Dutch Boy created its Twist and Pour paint can.[6] Until then, the consumer had an ever-increasing selection of colors, finishes, and even benefits such as environmentally friendly options. Yet the basic experience of opening the paint can, pouring it into a tray, and closing it was frustrating and messy—even for professionals. The "simple" solution had eluded many large and innovative organizations. The Twist and Pour can is made of plastic rather than metal, making it much lighter. It's easier for the retailer to mix the color and for the consumer to use because the lid comes off and can be closed tightly—keeping paint fresh longer. The spout prevents spilling, and the shape of the container means that retailers can stack

14 Twist and Pour containers where only 13 traditional paint cans would normally fit. It was a win for consumers, companies, and retailers. Despite the benefits, the old scenario remains the norm.

Similarly, in JBL's case, the answers that came about from investing in understanding the context of the consumer are quite different than the answers that would likely have emerged from the question, "How do I make a better speaker?" The latter would have perpetuated the focus on engineering that was already well recognized. The handles provided an opportunity to showcase engineering prowess that was visible to the consumer. Here, there was a happier ending—the EON was and continues to be a huge commercial success and a category leader. The right touch points can touch the heart—and can drive financial results.

Aside from a collaborative process and talented team, another key success factor was having some decision makers who "personify the consumers" within their ranks. JBL's Simon Jones was not only an audio engineer but also a musician. He understood and empathized with the target consumer on a level that would be difficult for an outsider, enabling him to make decisions based on firsthand experience. This intimate understanding also allows both sides to trust in the process and make better decisions because the immersion from both parties is genuine, not theoretical.

It's no surprise that the sectors that historically developed the most detailed use of personas and behavior were the ones that had to take on an incredible amount of risk: insurance, security agencies, and the military. Today, companies put their reputations on the line when they bring new products to market. Though information is gathered through observation and voluntary exchanges, here too personas are a powerful tool in mitigating risk. They also play an important role in uniting teams and developing strategies that result in positive emotional connections. The clarity and insight delivered through the use of personas creates a more efficient, effective development process.

Personification and Empathy in Practice

The idea of learning from consumers isn't new; however, the methods for yielding valuable and actionable insights have changed, especially where new products are concerned. Surveys and consumer satisfaction ratings can't always point the way to improved offerings. Here are some ways that companies are learning about their consumers:

Seeing with the Consumer's Eyes

When Tesco's Fresh and Easy supermarkets were studying the grocery store landscape in the United States, it didn't just purchase reports. The executive team lived with more than 200 families and looked at their frequency of shopping, where food was stored in the home, and why different outlets were used. As it developed the store concepts, a live shopping experience with fully stocked shelves was created. Immersion in real settings—for both executives and consumers—was key to achieving the right mix of prices, products, and shopping experience. Procter & Gamble CEO A. G. Lafley also does similar visits a few times a year, and P&G managers do so on a much more frequent basis. Disney has a team of anthropologists who carefully examine trends among teenage boys, looking for a way to tap the $50B in spending they represent and replicate the success of Disney franchises with teenage girls, such as Hannah Montana.[7]

Give Consumers a Chance to Create Their Own Personas

Many thriving companies today are not creating products per se, they're giving consumers a platform to craft their own personas. Whether it's social networking avatars, websites to build custom e-cards, video game and cartoon characters, or entire virtual worlds, consumers buy into the idea of trying on new personas and identities.

Match Your Consumers and Staff

When you know who your consumers are, it's that much easier to serve them by letting them interact with those who have a natural empathy. Some financial services firms hired baby boomers to answer calls from consumers distraught with losses in their retirement accounts. Having temporary workers on staff with the life experience and patience to understand consumer's anxiety helped reassure many callers.[8]

Design for Complex and Contradictory Impulses

When observing people in a dynamic fashion, be prepared for contradictions. Food manufacturers need to design for a desire for indulgence *and* health. Technology companies need to provide more features *and* simpler interfaces. Fashion designers need to provide great looks *and* low prices. Transforming persona insights into design requires a delicate balance of responding to rational and emotional triggers.

5

Own the Opportunity

Identifying emerging opportunities requires understanding gaps in which consumer emotions and desires are not met by current industry offerings; this reveals a new, uncontested market space. This leads to specific design priorities for target personas to guide the development process and maximize market share.

On a Wing and a Startup Prayer

In 2007, startup Vestalife debuted with the introduction of the Ladybug iPod speaker dock created and designed by LDA. The engaging little device got its name because it looks like a ladybug—the friendly little insect seen as a sign of good luck in many cultures. When closed, the Ladybug is a sphere a mere 5 inches in diameter. But with its "wings" unfurled, the speakers span a full 13 inches. The engaging character and design of the Ladybug struck an ideal balance between *playful* and *sophisticated*. By so doing, the Ladybug connected with the primary target market of younger kids, yet still appealed to adults looking for an out-of-the ordinary speaker dock.

Among hundreds of offerings in the crowded category, the Ladybug stood out, quickly becoming a media darling as it won both an iLounge 2008 MacWorld Best of Show and a 2008 International Consumer Electronics Show (CES) Innovations Design and Engineering

Award. According to iLounge's editor-in-chief, Jeremy Horwitz, "Vestalife's Ladybugs...are the extremely rare 'more than the sum of their parts' iPod speakers.... This is, without question, one of the best iPod speaker designs we have seen in the past six years."[1]

Although this early success and attention was gratifying, it also presented a challenge: How could Vestalife best follow up on the Ladybug and capitalize on its growing brand recognition?

Although it's hard enough for a young business to generate its first success, it can be as hard, or *even harder*, to get that second hit...to prove that the first "win" wasn't just a matter of "ladybug" luck. After all, 50 percent of all new businesses fail in their first 5 years.[2] But it's not just startups who fumble follow-up offerings—witness Motorola's inability to build on the success of the Razr.

For startups looking to repeat initial success, the game changes measurably from the initial toiling in anticipation of its first release. After delivering a hit, the barrier for entry has been lowered, but the risk is higher. In the early stages, entrepreneurs may be risking every cent they own. Later, they are also risking the brand equity built with the first hit. Vestalife founder Wayne Ludlum wanted more than one break-out hit; he was determined to build an enduring brand. It was a classic test of the adage "once you're lucky, twice you're good." His follow-up to the Ladybug would determine Vestalife's ultimate success or failure.

Understanding a Changing Landscape

When Vestalife was looking to create its next line of products, the market was rapidly changing. Speaker docks for iPods were just one of the major categories of products that were created from the phenomenal success of Apple's iconic MP3 player. In this crowded category, the iPod was the clear leader, and the accompanying iTunes store only amplified its success. By mid-2008, Apple announced that more than 5 *billion* songs had been downloaded in the 5 years since the iTunes store began operation.[3] Earlier the same year, iTunes surpassed Walmart as the largest music distributor in the United States.[4] The iPod line of media players went from a widely recognized design success to a huge commercial one as well—boasting global sales of 220 million units.[5]

There was no question that plugging into the iPod ecosystem was a big opportunity. However, a host of competitors and Apple itself were eager to take advantage of the growing market in accessories related to the iPod. To make an impact, Vestalife would need to create a design that could hold its own next to a design leader such as Apple. It also had to do so by creating a niche that could help Apple, one of the most marketing-savvy companies in the world, connect with an important audience.

The MP3 player market attracted a broad range of consumers including professionals, commuters, and fitness enthusiasts. At the same time, the character of the online music market was maturing and trends once driven by teenagers were migrating to older age groups. Furthermore, a majority of the traffic on music sites—56%—now comes from women.[6]

As early as 2006, the tech industry began to show an inflection point and the power of women in the technology sector became more apparent. In coining the term "Tech Fatales," *Microtrends* authors Mark Penn and E. Kinney Zalesne highlighted the following trends about female technology consumers:

> "Women outspend men on technology 3 to 2, and influenced 57% of technology purchases (about $90 Billion) in 2006. They pointed out that girls were more likely than boys to use mobile phones, digital cameras, satellite radios, and DVD recorders. *The only category where girls were lagging was in the Portable MP3 player* and videogame console markets. He concludes, "In study after study, women express different priorities, different preferences, and different concerns regarding technology. They want their gadgets light, durable,

and effective—not fast, sharp, and zillion-faceted...girls and women are deeply open to technology as fashion....

"Someday soon, someone is going to come along and tap into a fundamentally different way, and walk off with not just a niche market, but the largest and fastest growing piece of the tech puzzle. If you are a Tech Fatale, you are not alone...you are just waiting for someone out there to hear you."[7]

Penn and Zalesne point to hits such as the Wii and Dell's design revamp as examples of technology specifically designed to appeal to both genders. The early success of the Ladybug gave Vestalife a taste for the value of looking out for new consumers. However, its early choice of market was too specialized to create a mass-market success. Going forward, the company and the design team knew a few things for sure: The new offering had to connect with a female audience, yet appeal to young men as well; the Apple store channel was critical for success and visibility; and the new offering had to allow for personal expression in the same way that downloading your own songs did.

Finding the Opportunity for Follow-Up

Vestalife knew their second-year offerings had to more than live up to Ladybug's initial promise as it sought to expand its product line. To do this, Vestalife enlisted our team to help them identify and connect with new opportunities in the market.

Psycho-Aesthetics® mapping of the competitive landscape for iPod speaker docs revealed current offerings consisted of products whose design language was largely defined by black and white, rectangular, flat shapes. Most of the competition was still following Apple instead of the consumer and drawing inspiration from the iPod design for the accessories.

The team then examined the universe of iPod users. Ladybug had targeted younger kids and tweens, one category of underserved consumers. The remaining options in the market appealed largely to an older, more pragmatic, and mostly male audience, with spare aesthetics and a clear reference to technology. But in the upper-right quadrant, there was a clear opportunity to keep the original Ladybug audience engaged as they matured and begin to draw in older demographics who wanted more sophistication. The primary targets of teenage girls and young women were chosen, with young men as secondary targets. Young men already had some existing product offerings that were designed for them. A common thread among all the target consumers was the need to stand out in a crowd and the desire to express their individuality. With this understanding firmly in mind, the team set a manifest to create designs to connect not just with iPods, but also with the targeted iPod users.

Though Vestalife had planned to develop only one speaker dock follow-up in 2009, it fell in love with two separate preliminary designs: Firefly and Mantis. The Firefly design presents an intriguing, organic shape in sophisticated style that would hold appeal for both the male and female targets, as shown in Figure 5.1. Mantis, on the other hand, was designed to connect more deeply with the identified female personas, as shown in Figure 5.2. This design drew inspiration from the famed Fabergé eggs, known for their artistry, rich detail, and for the promise of a hidden surprise.

Both designs built on the original Ladybug. Angled, hidden hinges enable Firefly speakers to open, not just to the sides, but also moving slightly forward, in a welcoming posture. Mantis opens like a jewelry box to reveal the "hidden magic" of the speakers and the iPod dock.

On both systems, interchangeable faceplates were created in which consumers could embellish the speaker dock. This enabled users to customize their Firefly to help communicate their own personal passions. This interchangeable faceplate option also enables Vestalife to continue powerful cross-pollinations like the ones they conducted with Element Skateboards and luxury retailer Henri Bendel. The need for personalization was addressed, and an important secondary market was created—custom decal designs made by artists that can be used to embellish the faceplate.

© RKS Design

Figure 5.1   Vestalife Firefly (designer's rendering)

© RKS Design

Figure 5.2   Vestalife Mantis

As a result of its research, the team saw more opportunities to connect with this new audience. A product proliferation plan was developed to create headphones and earbuds that built on the design language and attributes of the speaker docks. Our designers realized that this could provide maturing Vestalife consumers a continuing connection to the brand.

The designs created were targeted to style-conscious young women, and the intent was to bring the appeal of fashion and jewelry to this category. Mapping of competitor products, which were largely sporty or technology driven designs, confirmed the strategic opportunity to bring higher fashion to the headphone and earbud markets. These designs would require a classic elegance to connect emotionally with these fashion-forward young trendsetters.

When you think of headphones and fashion, there is an immediate clash. Most headphones ruin hairstyles. Our designers took this age-old problem and turned it into a solution. With its built-in fashion headband, the Pi headphone becomes part of the hairstyle and has fabric-covered, interchangeable headband inserts. This enables people to express their individuality by how they choose to personalize their headphones. The insert can easily be swapped out, so users can match their headphones to their style or look for the day. For the earbuds, the team created three designs, each with its own style, all of them looking less like earbuds and more like earrings, as shown in Figure 5.3.

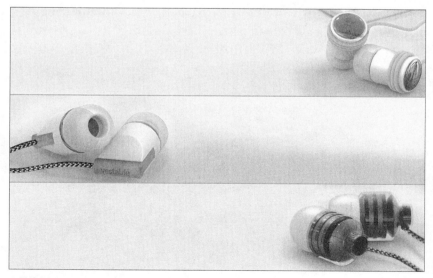

© RKS Design

Figure 5.3   Scarab, Boa, and Bumblebee earbud designs (top to bottom)

Taking a cue from high fashion, all three styles feature the embossed Vestalife logo in a prominent location. With more traditional earbuds, the design stops at the body. With Bumblebee, Scarab, and Boa, the team chose to bring attention to the cord, treating it, too, like jewelry that was meant to be displayed, not hidden. By wrapping the cord in fabric, it is transformed from an unsightly piece of electronics into something that evokes the look and feel of a necklace. Every aspect of the Vestalife earbuds are meant to be seen, not just heard. Finally, because these earbud designs are based in fashion, offering a "family" of three earbuds encourages buyers to get multiple sets for multiple looks.

A Market Winning Strategy

In sneak previews, the Pi headphones and the Bumblebee, Scarab, and Boa earbuds have piqued press interest and garnered retailer pre-orders far in excess of projections (see Figure 5.4). These designs combined with Firefly and Mantis help Vestalife place not only the iPod speakers, but also all its products in Apple stores worldwide.

© RKS Design

Figure 5.4   Pi headphones

Opportunity Is Where You Find It

For Vestalife, plugging into the Apple product civilization offered the best opportunity for the small company to have a chance at long-term success. This understanding informed the choices it made along the way. As resources and target consumers become more abundant, the choices are not always so clear-cut. The first step to capitalizing on an opportunity is to find it. Successful innovation requires identifying the right consumers, strategies, *and* designs. It is inefficient and usually ineffective to address these challenges as separate tasks. Crafting a coherent strategy becomes easier and less risky when consumers and competitive offerings are evaluated in concert. Doing so reveals *what is lacking in the market based on personality and emotional needs*. This gap in the competitive landscape that is populated by consumers with unmet needs and aspirations is what we call the Opportunity Zone. The Opportunity Zone is the result of combining insight about markets and consumers to discover unmet needs. This enables for the creation of experiences that capture consumer imagination as they capture market share.

The Benefits of Mining the Gaps

The innovation process is and always will be a process of discovery. However, given the time and effort required to bring a concept to market, it shouldn't be a matter of chance. The beauty (and benefits) of mining the gaps represented by opportunity zones are many-fold. Using Psycho-Aesthetics to find and connect with unserved consumers laser-focuses the development process, creates deeper connections with consumers, and reveals new paths for innovation.

- **Focusing the development process**—Bill Cosby once said, "I don't know the key to success, but the key to failure is trying to please everybody." Although Cosby may be an unlikely business sage, he makes a valid point. Trying to please all consumers will only lead to the development of products that are met with resounding indifference. Setting too many design priorities wreaks havoc with both the process and the result.

On the other hand, a clear and compelling vision can bring the impossible within reach. For example, the Tata Nano saw a global opportunity in creating a $2,000 car; MySpace created a platform for teenagers seeking both to define themselves and belong to a community; and the Flip camcorder won by introducing a new level of simplicity and a better consumer experience. Understanding the desired goals and outcomes establishes a clear target that all parties can aim for *before* the development process begins.

- **Connecting with consumers**—You can't connect with consumers until you know who they are. After you identify who falls into the Opportunity Zone, it's a fairly simple step to get to "how" to connect with them. In fact, you've already identified how to connect with each of your personas. Determining how to connect with the subset of personas in the Opportunity Zone is a straightforward process of identifying the common traits and triggers among those in the target user groups.

- **Creating an actionable manifest**—The length of most product development cycles demands that the insights from the mapping process be translated into an actionable manifest. This ensures that the goals for the design can be widely understood by design and executive teams alike. The manifest should enable flexibility in terms of the approach and yet clarity in terms of objectives. The actionable manifest is co-created with all stakeholders as the Opportunity Zone is revealed. The broad strategic priorities that can be understood at this early stage are the following:

  - **New consumers**—Uncovering potential new consumers is an important source of opportunity whether the market is an established or emerging one. Consider the social networking platform MySpace. Its growth was driven by teenagers using the sites to communicate with friends. However, newer communication sites and devices such as FaceBook, Twitter, and iPhones have multigenerational appeal.[8] When new customers have been identified, insights from their personas can drive innovation efforts.

- **New channels**—Day-in-the-Life Scenarios that include habits, preferences, and time spent in different channels can establish a basis for understanding new ways in which desired segments can be reached. Is the buying experience the pain point in adoption? Do people need a chance to learn about the product and test it before they will consider buying it? Will offering the product in certain channels dilute or increase the appeal and credibility of the design? Answering these questions for the target personas is critical in understanding the Opportunity Zone.

- **New business models**—When Netflix identified an untapped segment of users who liked to watch movies but hated the hassle of returning videos and paying late fees, they drove adoption by creating an innovative paid subscription model with no late fees.

  In the TV industry, executives are learning to supplement falling advertising revenues with product placement deals that counter the Tivo-effect of fast-forwarding through commercials and finding creative ways to tap into ancillary markets. The smartest writers even identify such opportunities when pitching new shows. *Glee*, a series about an underdog glee club, generates additional revenues through iTunes sales of songs performed by the cast on the show. And ABC's *Castle* has pushed the envelope even further with the actual publication of the book "written" by the fictitious author in the series. What's brilliant about this particular move is that it's not just a way to earn more from the series. It's also a way to connect more deeply with the audience. Until now, TV audiences shared experiences with each other. With this book, they can share experiences with characters in the series. It's a new business model that amplifies the consumer's emotional connection with the series.

To find opportunities for innovation beyond technology, look to see if target consumers have evolved beyond current offerings in the segment. What are the orthodoxies about business models in your industry? What are the assumptions about distribution, channels, and margins? Examine whether these are truly a response to the needs and preferences of the end users or merely an established practice. If the latter is true, there may be significant opportunities to create innovative new solutions for your target consumers.

Unearthing the Opportunity

In Chapter 3, "Map the Future," we learned how to map the competitive landscape of products or services based on consumer experience. In Chapter 4, "Personify Your Consumer," we mapped personas. Now it's time to put that work together to reveal the Opportunity Zone. Because both products and consumers are mapped on the same X–Y grid, this is accomplished by overlaying the persona and product maps to see which consumers connect with which products. The process can be seen in practice using our cell phone example, as shown in Figure 5.5.

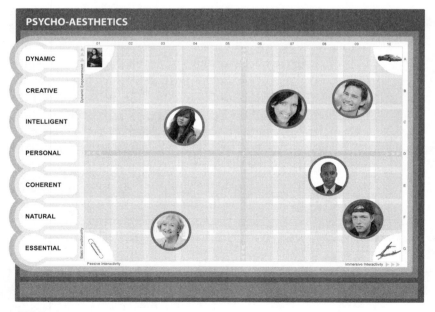

© RKS Design

Figure 5.5   Persona map of the cell phone market

Here we revisit the persona map of the cell phone market that shows both the level of interaction and experience that they are seeking in a cell phone (see Figure 5.6). Based on their needs, lifestyles, and personalities, we have a good idea of what they are looking for and purchasing in terms of features and pricing as well as their behavior in other categories (assembled from Day-in-the-Life and other persona tools).

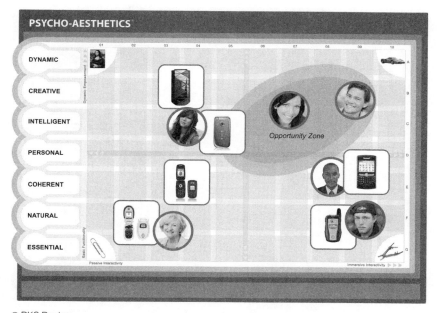

© RKS Design

Figure 5.6   Opportunity Zone for the cell phone market

The Opportunity Zone is where you find personas with no products that satisfy their needs. These personas represent classes of consumers who may be very different but still have overlap in their needs, desires, and aspirations—though likely to different degrees and for different reasons. For example, an interest in organic food may be shared by upper-income professionals, new parents, and eco-centrics. These are very different types of consumers, but they share an overarching concern for health.

When the maps of personas are overlaid with the existing products in the cell phone market, most of the consumers have at least
some products that suit their needs and personalities, as shown in
Figure 5.7. However, Sabrina and Tim don't have products that offer
anything that really engages them. These consumers may own a cell
phone but are likely among the hordes of "satisfied" consumers who
would defect if there were a better option. Kylie, the style-driven
consumer, may also seek out an alternative if it allowed her to connect
socially and looked attractive—but she is a secondary target.

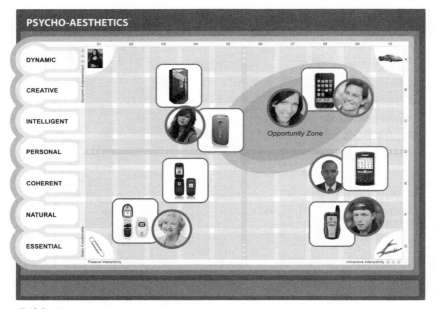

© RKS Design

Figure 5.7   From Opportunity Zone to winning design

Here we can see how identifying an Opportunity Zone can create
the insight that opens new markets. The combination of styling, computing, and function adds up to a level of interaction and experience
that never existed before. The product resonates with the target personas and likely many others as well. If the interface is simple enough
and the price point attractive, Mary in the Basic quadrant might be
interested. If the product is reliable enough, Trent and Joseph might

acquire a second device. A product that answers the needs of the target personas deftly will usually gain an audience outside of it as well.

When you have identified your target personas, you can reference back to their triggers and key attractors to develop an aggregate set of Key Attractors to drive the design process. By prioritizing the needs of the various personas, we can selectively combine their key attractors to appeal to more than one consumer at a time.

Choosing the Right Opportunities

Few companies would argue with the idea of connecting with consumers. The difficulty lies in figuring out how to do this. Consider the recurring lessons from research about how consumers think and make decisions: Consumers are looking for meaning. The product is the marketing. It's all about the experience. Complicating the picture is the fact that consumers are often unable to explain their purchase decisions.

Identifying the Opportunity Zone is therefore more complex than seeing an unmet need. There will always be more opportunities than resources. Deciding on a direction requires self-knowledge and consumer insight. Think about where your company can compete credibly, enthusiastically—and profitably. Many companies can and do compete successfully by improving and innovating where there are existing consumers and products. Even if this is the decision that is ultimately made, understanding where there may be uncontested opportunities and unmet consumer needs is still important. The learning from these personas can still provide insight and a sense of where the future lies.

In cases where a clear strategic direction seems elusive, or numerous targets are attractive, teams should ask—and build consensus—around the following questions:

- Who are the core consumers (both in terms of demographics and psychographics)? Who is at the fringes? Who is likely to adopt?
  Finding core consumers has become significantly more complex as consumers have gained more choices than at any point in human history. As Darrel Rhea of Cheskin observes,

"Designing today for a global market can mean trying to develop empathy for people in twenty countries...." When debating concepts that have a global reach, price points and benefits need to be considered at ever-earlier stages of development. Winning companies such as Target focus their efforts on women but their appeal extends far beyond.

- What is the main consumer pain point this solution is intended to solve? Will solving this problem create an opportunity for sustained market share?

As anyone who has watched a late-night infomercial knows, not every consumer problem represents a genuine market opportunity. If there are pain points that prevent large numbers of people from adopting, these should be prioritized. Can the solution *radically* reduce time and cost or increase fun and enjoyment? And if so, for how many target personas? How much of a market does each persona represent?

- What are the emotional benefits that the solution needs to deliver?

There must be a clear benefit for each persona that the team is aiming for. In addition to a great product or service, what other benefit is the consumer deriving emotionally? Microfinance offers those who make small loans the chance to see their investment doing good and improving lives around the world. How is sustainability addressed? The more levels on which the offering can empower the consumer, the better.

In identifying the Opportunity Zone, clarity counts. As Simon Fleming-Wood of Pure Digital Technologies said, "Strategy is also about knowing what you *won't* do." Consider AOL's famous directive to its developers years ago to "make it so easy your Grandma could use it." The market has changed dramatically since then, but technology developers know not to forget about Grandma. Florence Henderson of the Brady Bunch is creating the FloH Club, a tech support hotline that caters to seniors eager to get connected and understand their new devices. "You no longer have to endure your children or grandchildren rolling their eyes or getting exasperated with you," Henderson explained.[9] You can stay connected with your family.... And you don't have to feel embarrassed or stupid about asking for help."

The True Power

After you use Psycho-Aesthetics to find opportunity zones to identify and connect with consumers, you can find it hard to imagine working any other way. It provides the focus, insight, and consensus needed to reliably create breakout solutions.

All development teams need to increase the efficiency, mitigate risk, and find new opportunities for innovation. Identifying the Opportunity Zone aims to do all this and provide something even more valuable: connection.

Seeing how both markets and consumers are evolving—*on the same map*—is critical. The Opportunity Zone enables teams to understand unmet needs and gives them a means to test ideas about how to address them. The process of mapping opportunity zones and debating alternatives should result in the identification of a strategic direction and a set of broad design priorities.

Stakeholders should also come away with a clear idea of which consumers are the focus of each stage of product proliferation. For Vestalife, capturing the audience of young women was critical to building the brand and staking out a largely uncontested market space. Knowing that there were other segments with some overlapping needs for self-expression guided the design process. New features, aesthetics, and a personalization platform allow for crossover appeal.

An understanding of the critical channels that can enable connection with target personas should be established early in the development process. For Vestalife, the must-have channel was the Apple store. By providing a design that complemented the aesthetics of the iPod, Vestalife maximized the impact of its product by getting it in front of the most receptive audience. The company knew that its pricing and manufacturing had to support placement in this channel and crafted a business model around that.

The real power of opportunity zones lies in understanding where your target consumers have thus far been left out. They've been yearning for solutions that they can truly connect with. And they just aren't out there. Somehow, the market missed them. Whether they've evolved beyond current offerings or they were simply skipped over, these consumers are out there...ready and waiting for your development team to understand them. To hear their desires and aspirations. To deliver on their dreams. Opportunity Zones can help you see where they are and identify the means to reach them.

Three Essential Questions

Brainstorming the benefits that can attract various personas generates many new options—and confusion can come along with it. Many times, strategies falter because teams get "seduced by differences"[10] and end up diluting their focus and potential impact. In developing Psycho-Aesthetics, cognitive anthropologist Bob Deutsch collaborated with RKS to develop a universal framework to describe the thought process of consumers as they navigate the marketplace. Through extended discussions with Dr. Deutsch, we connected the dots between Psycho-Aesthetics and the experiential storytelling that draws a consumer's attention to specific design attributes. Dr. Deutsch explains that people ask three simple questions (subconsciously) with regard to visual stimuli:

Is it like me? The journey begins with the consumer seeing the new design for the first time. If the design is inviting, the consumer wants to interact with it, tentatively at first, but then is encouraged by the mentor (in this context, the design itself) to touch it.

Does it like me? The consumer thus crosses over the first threshold of his journey, where he encounters tests of usability and establishes connections with the design.

Can it make me more? The consumer explores the design further, in which his discovery and understanding of the design is enough for him to conclude that it can benefit him, and he seeks the rewards of ownership.

Identifying how to reach target consumers is largely a matter of answering these three questions through the design.

Part I Conclusion

"We're tired of talking about strategy," is a comment we hear with increasing frequency. "We know what the competition is doing; we know the trends. Can you please just show us the designs?" This frequent request confirms the growing importance of design in corporate strategy and the changing nature of competition. Today, competition is no longer just about creating insight to guide strategy; it is also about *demonstrating* that insight in superior designs.

Great companies have always been in the design business, whether they say so explicitly. Creating new products, services, and experiences—and emotional connections in the process—is key to the growth of companies and brands. These connections are not a matter of a single aesthetic but a way of understanding the needs and aspirations of consumers. Design today must carry through from a corporate philosophy about consumer experience to inform strategy and implementation.

As Plato once said, "The beginning is the most important part of the work." *The starting points of the design process have a powerful impact on the final outcome.* Understanding the emotional triggers for different consumers should be an explicit goal of stakeholders from the outset. Otherwise, the dynamics within companies and in the marketplace can make adoption elusive regardless of the merits of a new concept. Therefore, the challenge of adopting a new concept is not only to overcome trained behavior but also to *motivate* new behavior. Design isn't the biggest part of what designers do; it's simply their tool to create cause and effect. And it isn't about how the consumers feel about the design; it is all about how the design makes them feel about *themselves*. Design strategy succeeds when it can address the emotional needs—and hurdles—of consumers as it delivers on quality, function, and price. That said, companies can radically reduce time to market and mitigate risk by focusing on just a few priorities:

- **Reduce complexity.** Few companies can innovate by collecting *more* demographic data, financial projections, or anecdotal information. To be clear, we are not suggesting that data should be ignored; however, in the absence of a consumer context, the data can provide distraction without direction.

- **Establish the consumer experience as the basis of collaboration.** Framing the design process in the context of the consumer breaks down organizational silos and allows everyone the opportunity to participate. Everyone is a consumer and can contribute insight about how the user experience can be improved. Understanding how empowerment varies among personas and evolves over time can help to create priorities and inform design and investment decisions.

- **Use maps to guide the way.** Mapping products and personas in terms of needs, desires, and aspirations fuels the design process with clarity and empathy from the outset. This is not only a powerful tool for understanding how to appeal to consumers, but it can also shape the debate about trade-offs that are an inherent part of implementation. Deep consumer insight can reveal whether what is being eliminated is the equivalent of trimming a toenail or removing a vital organ. The visual understanding provided by Psycho-Aesthetics® mapping can provide a reality check and a benchmark throughout the design and innovation process.

There is no ideal location on the map that companies must drive toward. The direction should be determined by the needs of consumers and the particular company's strategy. There are cases of highly profitable and well-loved companies in every quadrant. What they have in common is an ability to see where there is a disconnect between the offerings in the market and the desires of consumers are and create winning designs to bridge the gap.

- **Aim for a compass, not a GPS.** Identifying the Opportunity Zone can increase the chances of success by focusing a team's attention on a finite number of priorities. These form the basis for experimentation during the design process. The idea is to provide a clear direction but allow freedom to all parties to generate different approaches.

Reflecting on the cases that we've covered thus far, we can reflect on the role that the design played in moving each company toward its strategic objectives. All the efforts helped the companies connect (or reconnect) with consumers as they delivered financial results. Psycho-Aesthetics enables companies to understand how markets and consumers are evolving, but it can also be a valuable forensic tool. The Opportunity Zone can be anywhere on the map—depending on industry dynamics.

Amana

Here, Psycho-Aesthetics was focused on aesthetic changes to enhance consumer experience. It was also done under cost and time constraints. Amana had fallen into the commodity trap in consumers' eyes despite high quality, largely due to its poor design (see Figure A). By selecting designs that enhanced consumer experience and reflected important changes in lifestyles, Amana separated from the pack by moving from a commodity to an enriched offering. The shift enabled Amana to reconnect with women, who often drove purchase decisions, and the image of the brand was raised to the standard of the quality inside. The new line made people feel like better nurturers and caretakers. At the time, Maytag was the industry leader, and acquired Amana soon after its brand revival.

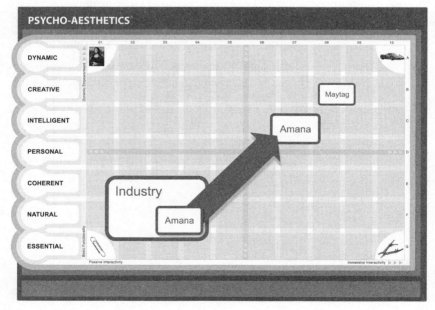

© RKS Design

Figure A   Psycho-Aesthetics map of Amana industry positioning

Flip Cam

The Flip camcorder was not designed by our firm, but it stands out as a great example of changing the industry by re-imagining the consumer experience (see Figure B). Here, the idea of transforming the consumer experience inspired the development process from concept to execution. The company knew the benefits that they wanted to deliver and focused their design efforts accordingly. Although most of the offerings in the category were adding features (many of them were in the Versatile quadrant) and growth was tapering off, Flip Video expanded the market by simplifying the operation and adding style. Women, college students, and those intimidated by traditional video cameras could enter the market, and a significant number of consumers purchased a Flip cam as a second device when they didn't want to do an elaborate setup. The new design made people feel confident about taking video and made sharing it easy and fun.

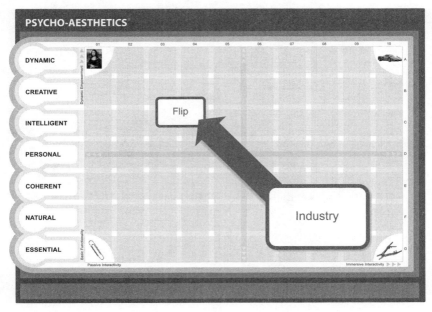

© RKS Design

Figure B   Psycho-Aesthetics map of Flip Video industry positioning

JBL Professional

JBL Professional's story with the EON line of speakers is a classic case of an innovation whose value eroded over time and had to be refreshed. The original EON was far ahead of its competitors, but the gap between offerings had narrowed. JBL had to create a design that conveyed its superior quality and its lightweight technology (see Figure C). The company regained its market position and connected with a wide range of people who made their living from music.

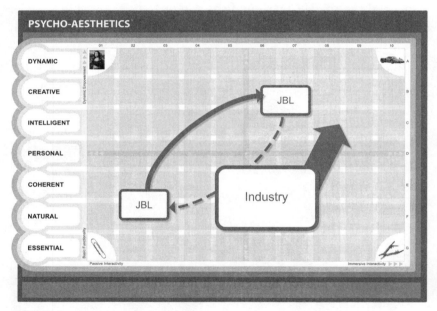

© RKS Design

Figure C   Psycho-Aesthetics map of JBL Professional industry positioning

Vestalife

Vestalife entered a crowded category by being the first to create an iPod speaker dock specifically for young girls who were identified as a group of consumers with unmet needs. Vestalife's initial design was artistic. As a result of its use of a Psycho-Aesthetics fueled design, it a) created a product proliferation strategy, b) expanded the opportunity zone to include more personas and c) gained entry into a coveted sales channel. The offerings allowed people to express their individuality as they enjoyed the function and aesthetics of the iPod (see Figure D).

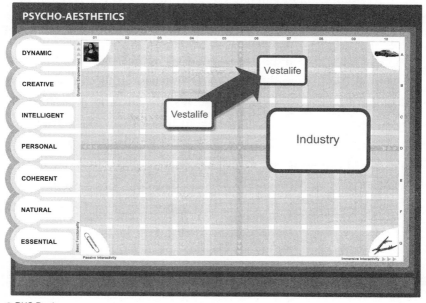

© RKS Design

Figure D   Psycho-Aesthetics map of Vestalife industry positioning

Aligning stakeholders around a design strategy is critical for success. Many of the poor designs we see are a result of poor collaboration, not a lack of design expertise. A designer's sketch and a manager's pro forma spreadsheet essentially serve the same purpose: to provide a vision of what the future may look like. Until the results are in, it's hard to judge who has the right idea. And the disparate lenses of managers and designers *can* make it hard to achieve understanding and consensus in the design process. Although marketing and accounting departments can share their numbers and understand each other, with designers and managers the transparency must be created with tools and interaction. And that transparency is essential for giving companies the confidence to make bold decisions and enter new markets. Design is not the strategic risk; on the contrary, it can be the strategic insurance—a way to make sure that investments are rewarded in the marketplace.

Part II, "Implementation and Consumer Experience," covers how the design strategy can be executed effectively. The actual prototyping and feedback process, calibration, and consumer testing are explored in depth. We illustrate with various case studies how the emotional insight can be manifested in actual designs. Carrying through on the philosophy that market success is about how design makes consumers feel about themselves, we illustrate how to draw inspiration from Joseph Campbell and use the "hero's journey" to frame the purchase decision and create the "moment of truth" for the consumer. Putting it all together creates "predictable magic"— market success for companies and empowerment for consumers.

Part II

Implementation and Consumer Experience

6

Work the Design Process

Translating research and insight into actual design is where firms can monetize their strategies. A purely statistical interpretation of research is a bit like driving while looking only in the rear- and side-view mirrors. Armed with the maps of the industry, personas, and Opportunity Zone, we can see the road ahead.

With our mapped insights for inspiration, we work through the design process: create, test, re-create, re-test, and so on. As we work through this process, we are guided through this iterative cycle by our understanding of the emotional connections we seek to create for our personas. We are now empowered to create and innovate.

As James Dyson, creator of the top-selling upright vacuum cleaner in the United States and the richest industrial designer in the world notes: "Everyone has ideas. They may be too busy or lack the confidence and technical ability to carry them out."[1] Success doesn't come easily even to those, like Dyson, who possess the required traits. The importance of persistence can be seen in his story. It took more than 5,127 prototypes, long years of indebtedness, and several lawsuits before Dyson's vision became a market success. What began with scissors and duct tape ultimately cemented his global reputation as an inventor.

Whether the design process begins as a result of a strategic initiative or a personal inspiration, the path to realizing the vision is remarkably similar. However, a great design doesn't always translate into business success. The stakes for declaring a design success have moved considerably. It used to be that handing over a promising rendering was the end goal. Then a model was needed to help teams visualize and later, fully functioning prototypes with engineering detail. Designers soon became involved with the details of production. Today, design strategy needs to illuminate a clear path laid out from the sketch to an empowered consumer. For this to happen, the realities of implementation—business models, distribution, and budgets—need to be integrated into the design process. Here, we share two stories of innovations that won awards and enhanced the lives of consumers. However, minute details of execution resulted in only one becoming a huge commercial success.

From a Guitar Stand to a Guitar

After observing that existing guitar stands were bulky, cumbersome things made of tubular metal and were awkward to use and unattractive to look at, the RKS design team was presented with a challenge: Design a better guitar stand. Jokingly, Project Manager Paul Janowski replied, "Why don't we design a better guitar?"

The idea was crazy enough to capture the imagination of everyone in the firm—including the nonmusicians. At the time, the electric guitar had been relatively unchanged for 50 years. It was a classic. An icon. How could a design firm with no musical pedigree meet the challenge? This wasn't an effort that would take a few days to mock up and refine. It would require taking complete responsibility for the design *and* business decisions in the development process. But the promise was exhilarating as well. Ravi's motivation was simple: "I was part of a generation that listened to rock and roll and thought of guitars as more than just instruments...guitars are social icons. They are the tools that enable poets and musicians to connect us through the universal language of music. The guitar was beyond this: a rare opportunity for a designer to create an artifact that can outlive them.[2]

That was the beginning of a long and inspiring design process: a constant cycle of creation, evaluation, and re-creation. Whether you're creating a song, story, service, or product, it takes the same love of the process, the same tenacity. From simple sketches to complex 3D renderings to proof-of-concept prototypes, the process involves trial and error and evaluating various approaches against the maps. Refinements are made continuously until the team identifies a solution that can resonate with consumers.

Set Up a War Room

The term *war room* has evolved from its initial, literal meaning to the modern business application: a collaborative space in which to focus on a specific goal. The iterative design process always includes the risk that, at some point in the revisions, the original objective will be lost. The predictable, repeatable success of the Psycho-Aesthetics® framework depends on the team's ability to refocus on the common goals established during the mapping process.

Whether you use a physical room, or a virtual suite of tools, the experience of a war room can transcend itself. A war room is truly greater than the sum of its components. Whether you collaborate across a table or across an ocean, the key ingredient is access to the visual tools created during the mapping process: the visual representations of the market, opportunity zones, the persona dashboards, and Day/Week-in-a-Life narratives. As you walk in, you are reminded or told of the stores of the brands and people and lives that will be affected by what you do. Imagine a 6-foot-tall line of posters, 20 feet long that encapsulates the five personas that represent variations in our target audience; on the opposite wall are all the Psycho-Aesthetic maps and Key Attractors. Regardless of the dimensions of your room or the size of your visualizations, having all the Psycho-Aesthetic materials together in one place is powerful. In this way, team members are immersed in the consumer context for their innovations and focused on the emotional connections they seek to create.

Uncovering Aspirations (of Guitar Players)

With RKS guitars, as with any project, the key was to begin with the individual. What single thread runs common to all electric guitar players? A desire to express their unique vision; a passion to share their singular point-of-view with the world. This longing wasn't limited to professional musicians. Market research confirmed that many adults who had been coaxed into more traditional careers still harbored a desire to be rock stars. Guitar sales more than doubled between 2000 and 2004, and Chinese imports lowered the price point for many entry-level guitars. Beginners and players who wanted to expand their instrument collection with additional guitars accounted for a large number of the new consumers—and market growth.[3]

How sadly ironic that, despite guitar players loving to push the envelope, electric guitar technology had been virtually stagnant for 50 years. Most of the innovations came from musicians and were rarely incorporated into mainstream designs because artists were eager to hold on to their trade secrets. One exception was Les Paul, the guitar prodigy and creator of the solid body electric guitar. He collaborated with guitar maker Gibson on instruments that shaped the industry for half a century. As legend has it:

> "In 1940 or 1941—the exact date is unknown—Mr. Paul made his guitar breakthrough. Seeking to create electronically sustained notes on the guitar, he attached strings and two pickups to a wooden board with a guitar neck. 'The log' as he called it, if not the first solid body electric guitar, became one of the most influential ones. The odd-looking instrument drew derision when he played it in public, so he hid the works inside a conventional looking guitar. But the log was a conceptual turning point...the beginning of a sonic transformation of the world's music.

"The Gibson company hired Mr. Paul to design a Les Paul model guitar in the early 1950s, and variations of the first 1952 model have sold steadily ever since, accounting at one point for half of the privately held company's total sales. Built with Mr. Paul's patented pick-ups, his design is prized for its clarity and sustained tone. It has been used by musicians like Led Zeppelin's Jimmy Page and Slash of Guns N' Roses. The Les Paul version is unchanged since 1958, the company says."[4]

By the dawn of the 21st century, there was clearly room for innovation in the market.

Although rock stars represent creativity and freedom to their fans, they are surprisingly traditional in their choice of instruments. The lead guitarist is often the band leader and most recognized artist in a band, whose reputation is on the line during every performance. They need guitars they can count on. Amateur electric guitar players have less on the line but often mimic their idols' choice of instruments. The heroic evangelists necessary for getting traction in this segment were already heroes (and rock stars) in their own right. To lure them to try something new, it would have to be a marked departure from what was already out there. If the potential benefits weren't considerable, there would be no motivation to explore the new design.

Get Started—Fast

The momentum and excitement of innovation can fade if some progress is not made relatively quickly. The team began with a thorough Psycho-Aesthetics analysis of the market, and with the challenges firmly in mind, devised a plan to address them. As they began work, they made sure that the designers included both guitar players and nonplayers. The novices were essential for the fresh perspective they brought. The musicians brought empathy and deep knowledge of the habits, preference, and pain points of the target audience.

Together, the team stripped the concept of a guitar down to its essentials: the resonance chamber or body for producing rich acoustics and the neck that's home to the fingerboard. Designers took this core concept and developed it into a "core instrument," crafting an innovative design in which the neck and resonance chamber melded into a slender core unit and combined with a bolted on open-architecture body suspended by ribs extending out from the core. This open architecture, combined with the slimness of the core (which is not much wider than the strings) gives the designers a wonderful opportunity to place the volume and tone controls just below the strings, right at the player's fingertips in the space between the core and the body shell. The pickup selector was placed in the opening just above the strings, within easy reach of the player's thumb. These innovative placements worked both to create an uncluttered design and to enhance ergonomics while allowing new moves for the player, such as changing pick-ups and rolling the volume between chords with great ease.

After hundreds of ideas and concept sketches, one design stood out. It combined the sumptuous curves of a female body and exposed structural ribs that evoked those of a human skeleton. It was neither a solid body nor a hollow body; it was an open-architecture hollow body with a neck through the center core. It was a design like nothing on the market, so it was sure to stand out. But the question was, would traditionalist guitar players be receptive? At this point in the design process, it was an idea that captivated everyone and provided the inspiration for further development and experimentation.

The Role of Experts/Lead Users

The core unit, open-architecture guitar design was a radical departure from tradition. The design team was excited about it, but knew they needed professional feedback if they were to develop this concept into a successful product. Luckily, Ravi's brother Ramesh was friends with Rock and Roll Hall of Fame inductee Dave Mason. Mason, a cofounder of the band Traffic, was known for his collaborations with George Harrison, Paul McCartney, Eric Clapton, Jimi Hendrix, and many others as well as his solo work. He was curious enough to stop by RKS to check out its first foam model. Although elements of the design (such as the core unit—construction) intrigued Mason, other features simply did not work for him. This original model lacked a headstock with tuning knobs; these were placed elsewhere. That was a no-go. Mason continued with his critique, giving the team a list of things that had to go, were missing, or needed refinement for the new design to become a "player's guitar."

Getting Started with Design—By Quadrant

For all the excitement involved in the creative process, getting started can be daunting. But after you identify the Opportunity Zone and where you want to be, you can focus on design priorities that appeal to the personas in each quadrant (see Figure 3.4 in Chapter 3). While the details of how to create a design that will stand out in each quadrant are category-specific, certain questions and general guidelines can keep the design process on track.

- **Basic quadrant**—Few designs are created explicitly for the Basic quadrant. Most often, designs are simplified and move toward this quadrant from elsewhere on the map as companies search for ways to broaden the audience and appeal of a successful product. For example, how can "designer" goods and complex gadgets be made more accessible—both in terms of cost and function?

  As designs are simplified for this quadrant, each feature is carefully considered. Successful basic products are not "dumbed-down" products. In many cases, they require a higher level of problem solving and creativity. The value of the product needs to be visible and appealing to a wide range of people, often at a lower cost.

Questions for teams in the Basic quadrant:

- Which features can be simplified or eliminated all together?
- Which details are confusing or difficult for large numbers of people?
- Which elements are essential to the brand identity and aesthetics?

- **Versatile quadrant**—In the Versatile quadrant, designs often serve multiple functions and must convey efficacy and performance. Many of the designs in this quadrant are for professional use and "gear," such as sports equipment. Here, an over-designed or overly attractive look often detracts from their appeal.

Design priorities should include avoiding *feature creep*—a great temptation in this quadrant. Predictability, reliability and ease of use are important, and material choices should be durable. Simple user interfaces often require high degrees of attention due to the complexity of the offering.

Questions for teams in the Versatile quadrant:

- Does each feature support the user's goals?
- Does the design have superior usability?
- Do the aesthetics convey the design's purpose? Is it pragmatic?

- **Artistic quadrant**—In the Artistic quadrant, beauty and aesthetics are central to the design's appeal. However, the design must to be more than just attractive; it must have a sense of exclusivity and provide individuals with an opportunity for self-expression. The best fashion and jewelry brands understand this—and designs in this category can be polarizing. Quirkiness and individuality are key attributes in this quadrant.

Questions for teams in the Artistic quadrant:

- How unique is this product? Does it help the users express themselves?

- Can this design be personalized?
- Which details of the design hold special value?
- **Enriched Quadrant**—In this quadrant are the designs that engage multiple senses and create memorable experiences. Here, substance and style are valued by consumers, and these elements need to be balanced in the design.

Questions for teams in the Enriched quadrant:

- How many senses are engaged by this design?
- Do the function and styling reach the same standard? Do they reinforce each other?

To many, this unvarnished feedback would have been disheartening. But to the designers this was exciting. Feedback is an essential part of the design process, and outside feedback from a recognized expert in the field is even *more* valuable. The gut-level reaction from someone of Mason's caliber and his interest motivated the team. So although Mason's notes sent them back to the virtual drawing board, this new understanding of the problems with the design provided direction to the development process.

Every iteration moves a design closer to reality. With the in-house capability to do design changes and Computer Numeric Control (CNC) working rapidly (to create new models), it was only a couple weeks before Mason's phone rang again. The team had another model ready for him to check out. Mason was surprised; frankly, he hadn't expected to hear from them again. He was even more surprised when he saw how much they accomplished in that short period of time. Mason could see the potential and knew they were onto something. Drawn by the excitement and pull of the iterative process, he and the design team kept at it for nearly two years, working the design process and constantly comparing their work against the foundation laid by Psycho-Aesthetics. As new information was brought in from working with Mason, personas, key attractors, and maps were further refined. When they moved into working prototypes, Mason began taking the guitars out on the road, using them in live performances to test and evaluate the positions of the knobs, neck, and body refinements, and more. Regarding the neck, the most critical point of engagement, Mason said, "There was one version where I knew it wasn't right...for me the judgments are very tactile." The team went back and checked its measurements and confirmed that they were off—by 1/100th of an inch! That amount of variation requires precise measurement tools to identify, but to a player like Mason who'd been playing 46 years, it was big enough to feel in his bones.

Mason became such an integral part of the process, and such a believer in the guitar, that he became a founding partner in RKS Guitars when it was formed as a separate entity. Mason's insight into the perspective and passion of professional musicians combined with Psycho-Aesthetics was an essential part of the design process.

Back to the Consumer

Ironically, the passion of designers and enthusiasts can derail a design by taking it too far away from the consumer's comfort level. Aesthetic improvements can begin to look superficial; new features can start to seem confusing. At critical points in the development process, a reality check is in order.

The question of which innovations are the most meaningful to consumers is never a simple one. Psycho-Aesthetics steers the team toward the most meaningful solutions as it navigates it through the design process.

For highly personal and customized concepts, the role of emotion grows more prominent. The guitar couldn't just be a test of design skills and creativity; it needed to provide a superior experience for rock stars, fans, and aspiring musicians alike. The focus had to be on sound quality, playing experience, and the rock-star image.

Sustainable Solution to Sound Quality

As the guitar moved from foam prototypes to working models, the team put a lot of time and consideration into manufacturability and materials. The tone wood used in most guitars often comes from endangered sources found in the rain forests. To eliminate the endangered tone woods required, the team looked at using molded plastic for the guitar bodies in combination with farm-raised woods. But the problem was that most plastic sounded "bright" and annoying. No one was prepared to compromise on sound quality.

Luckily, Eastman Chemical manufactured a cellulose-based polymer called Tenite. This was one of the first plastics ever created, based on the original materials founding company Eastman/Kodak used for creating photographic film. Eastman quickly proved to be excited about the promise of something as innovative as the new guitar being developed by the team. They sent samples of various formulations for sound testing.

The cotton and wood fiber in Tenite gave it an amazing resonance—a sound reminiscent of traditional tone woods used in musical instruments, yet still, very unique and desirable. Sourced from these sustainable materials, the Tenite was far more environmentally responsible than traditional tone woods. The structural ribs that remained from the original concept were crafted out of aircraft aluminum. These ribs worked synergistically with the Tenite, transmitting the vibrations from the strings, through the ribs, and into the molded shell. The use of this material meant that these RKS Hollow Body guitars would require no tone wood from environmentally sensitive rainforests, and other models reduced the use of tone wood by approximately 80 percent.

Optimized Ergonomics for a Better Playing Experience

The Psycho-Aesthetics analyses had identified control placement as an important touch/pain point. This told the team that there was an important opportunity to create differentiation by enhancing ergonomics, aesthetics, and the entire experience. The most obvious ergonomic innovations were optimal placement of the volume and tone knobs and the pick-up selector within the gaps above and below the core unit. The Groove Knobs, as the volume and tone knobs came to be known, were placed just below the strings at the player's fingertips. The knobs were weighted and finished with polished metal to evoke quality and enhance precision. The Posifly Pickup Selector was positioned within easy reach of the player's thumb to enable on-the-fly changes when wanted, yet keep it safe from unwanted mid-groove pick-up-change mishaps. But these control placements were just the beginning of the ergonomic improvements inherent in the design.

Everything from the neck and fingerboard through the shape of the guitar body was addressed. Most traditional electric guitar bodies have flat backs. But the sensual contours of the RKS guitar design extend to the back of the guitar, creating an incredible guitar-to-player connection. The way the guitar seemingly wraps around the player's body enables a much more relaxed, natural position and creates a stronger physical connection between guitar and player. Mason's input was integral in creating this fit. "[The guitar] had to allow me to forget about it; allow me to focus on my music and become an extension of my hands," he said. In this process, we dropped three pounds out of the guitar, which addressed a concern expressed by players who complained that competitor guitars hurt their backs after hours of extended play.

The Final Result

What mattered most was how the guitar was received by musicians. From first glance, veteran guitar players and novices alike commented on the guitar's visual presence. Some liked it; some rejected it. The design was polarizing, as we had planned it to be. From the start, we knew we would have to turn some people off to turn others on. We weren't designing a guitar for every player...we were designing to turn our personas into heroic evangelists. And we did.

Magic happened when people picked up the guitar. The first experience is one of comfort and familiarity. It was designed to feel like an old friend. As wildly new as it looked, it *felt familiar*. As players got more familiar with it, the benefits of intelligent, empathic design could be fully appreciated—the control placement, the note-to-note clarity and definition, the amazing resonance, and the obsessive craftsmanship. Suddenly, players of varying abilities began to feel like...rock stars. But the appeal of the guitar extended to the musical role models that inspired its creation. Perhaps this is the reason that Mick Jagger adopted the RKS guitar as his personal song-writing instrument and legions of legendary players, such as Glen Campbell, Don Felder, Keith Richards, Ron Wood, and Rickie Lee Jones, joined the RKS Guitar family.

Personalized Experience

Just as innovation can help you connect key targets, it can also help you connect with a wider audience. Though the original RKS guitars were adopted by many top players, they were too expensive for some. Our analysis revealed that the opportunity zone could be expanded and outlying personas could be brought into the fold. To do this, we would need to make the guitar affordable enough for aspiring musicians on a budget. The design team also set a goal to address unmet desires for individuality.

The solution was made possible by the core unit design that was the foundation of the original RKS guitar. The design team realized that the core unit's architecture enabled the development of interchangeable guitar bodies. The new guitar line, called the Wave (shown in Figure 6.1), gave players the option of switching out various guitar bodies to fit the mood or the music. With the use of just six screws, the player can create a completely different look and sound.

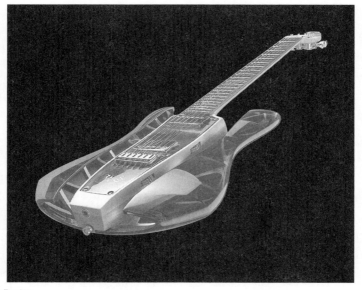

© RKS Design

Figure 6.1   RKS interchangeable body guitar

With the advent of the Wave, musicians could own an instrument that gave them the ability to change to match their mood, the venue, or even just their whims. The elimination of costs associated with the ribs helped make the interchangeable body guitars' line much more affordable. The option to have one core unit and multiple bodies meant that users could modify a single core unit to have different looks and sounds to create a virtual "stable" of guitars without having to pay the price of having multiple guitars.

The Importance of Execution

Our experience with RKS guitars gave us a visceral understanding of the complexity and details involved in execution. As the guitar was being developed, we hesitated to sell it to a manufacturer before we felt it was ready, knowing that the opportunity may not come again. As it grew into the vision we had, the thought of letting it remain a series of sketches and models that were taken on the road was unacceptable. After weighing many options, RKS took the very unusual step of forming a separate company, RKS Guitars, to manufacture the highly specialized instruments in Southern California.

When the factory opened its doors, the highly artistic process and training involved meant that almost ten people took a full day to produce a guitar. During the 3½ years of operations, this was reduced to about one guitar per person per day. Three guitar bodies were created utilizing the basic guitar core—the Solid Body, Hollow Body, and Wave—that could be assembled into approximately 200 SKUs. The guitars were sold online and in catalogs, with 80 domestic dealers and 30 international distributors. Breakeven was achieved and a 3-month backlog of orders was evidence of the appeal of the product.

Ultimately, however, the reliance on small specialty suppliers for many of the parts curtailed our ability to meet demand. We had to raise money to advertise the guitars, and suppliers were unable to extend credit. Although the team had put tremendous thought and effort into the user experience, it simply wasn't enough. The needs of the retailers were not adequately considered, and we underestimated the amount of cash required to build the brand. The importance of educating dealers about the benefits of the guitar was not given enough importance, especially in the larger chains. This was particularly difficult for the team who knew that the guitar was understood and appreciated by many consumers.

A great business model can sometimes compensate for a lackluster product, but a great design can seldom overcome business reality.

This was the case with RKS Guitars. Although the product was in high demand, there was inadequate funding to propel the brand and meet the demand we had generated. The company suspended production in 2007, but the 2,000 instruments produced are still in strong demand and continue to appreciate in price.

Channeling Our Learning

The experience with RKS Guitars forced us to be consistently explicit about understanding the dynamics of channels as we crafted design strategies. We had done so successfully in our work with Robert Hayman, CEO and co-founder of Discus Dental. He knew from experience the importance of having not just a good product, but the right image and design that would create viral demand. It was a lesson he learned early on in his family business. His father was the man behind the famous Giorgio of Beverly Hills fragrance brand. That experience shaped how he looked at all his later ventures. "The bold yellow and white stripes [on their packaging] just projected the image of Beverly Hills...it was distinctive and immediately recognizable. In a high-end market, it really becomes more and more about emotion," Hayman observed.[5]

When Hayman founded Discus Dental, with Dr. Robert Dorfman (a celebrity dentist often appearing on the popular TV show *Extreme Makeover*), the tooth-whitening market was in a period of rapid growth. Sales of oral care products had grown 19 percent from 1997 to 2002 to $4.5 billion in the United States. Whitening and breath freshening products accounted for much of this growth, and in the words of one analyst, "The shift in the market has gone from hygienic to more cosmetic in focus."[6] The American Academy of Cosmetic Dentistry reported a 300 percent increase in tooth-whitening procedures between 1995 and 2000.

After considering various ways to participate in the market, from infomercial formats to direct sales, Discus ultimately decided to target dentists' offices. Professional products such as BreathRx and Nite White (a kit with a mouth guard and whitening gel) were successfully launched in the channel. "We always knew we were in the cosmetics business, as well as the oral care business," Hayman recollects.

Designing a New Way to Market

As a young company, the traditional model of hiring experienced reps to visit dental offices was not financially feasible. However, Hayman insists that being underfunded was key to the company's success because it forced the company to be resourceful. The founders capitalized on a tough job market and hired fresh college graduates as its sales force and had many of them sell products over the phone. The high performers were asked to refer friends for employment as the company grew. The young, energetic reps were a hit at frequent trade shows and reinforced the association of Discus products with youth and sex appeal. Inside the company, the friendship and camaraderie among the salespeople fostered a strong work ethic. Here, too, emotional connections played a role in the company's growth.

At the time, a huge assortment of whitening products aimed at baby boomers was entering the grocery and drugstore aisles, from whitening strips to pastes and brush-on gels. These products appealed to many consumers in younger age groups as well. A Rembrandt spokeswoman explained, "White teeth have become a standard of beauty; the market is much broader than its original base."[7] Teeth were suddenly a high-stakes item in market for youth and sex appeal. Some industry surveys showed 71 percent of Americans saying that they were less likely to marry someone with bad teeth and 33 percent reporting that whitening was the main attribute they looked for in a toothpaste.[8] The retail channel offered convenience and lower prices than professional products, and Discus chose not to dilute the brand by following the trend.

However, the emergence of BriteSmile, a stand-alone franchise offering tooth-whitening in one hour and a system for dentists, posed the major threat to Discus. Hayman remembers vividly, "It was a time when we knew we had to win—that moment when you either capitulate or compete. We had to find a way to answer this threat."

But the company was already 2 years behind when it began its effort to counteract BriteSmile. Years of relationships with dentists led them to believe that a significant population of adults were interested in tooth whitening yet impatient with over-the-counter products. They were anxious about walking into a franchise such as BriteSmile. Discus again chose to leverage the valuable relationships it had built with dentists as the core of its strategic response. It began using Psycho-Aesthetics to develop a whitening system that could be performed in dentist's offices.

Competing by Helping Others Win

The result was the Zoom! tooth whitening system, which is a peroxide-based gel activated by an ultra-violet lamp to whiten teeth. The shape of the Zoom! whitening lamp, shown in Figure 6.2, was specifically designed to reduce patient's fears and anxiety. The aesthetic was created by separating the power supply pod from the lamp itself, making it far less intrusive and bulky. The lamp also increased patient safety because it is aimed at the treatment area and away from the patient's eyes.

The Zoom! system produced superior results of whitening teeth up to eight shades in an hour, at 30 percent of the cost of alternative patient therapies. The lamp won several design awards and was a stark contrast to the BriteSmile experience, in which a huge lamp was aimed at the patient, and they were cautioned to "stay as still as possible." Not moving was so critical to the BriteSmile system that motion sensors were installed to detect patient's shifting.

By giving dentists an opportunity to compete in a growing and lucrative market and make their patients feel wonderful in the process, Discus rapidly regained lost ground. Patients also had more chances to learn and discuss tooth whitening with a trusted source without feeling compelled to make a decision. When they were ready to have the procedure done, they usually opted to have it done in the doctor's office. Here, the design team worked with Discus to develop a sustainable business model and channel strategy instead of limiting their attention to the end user. The lamp and patented syringe designed for Discus gave dentists a reliable and cost-effective way to help their patients achieve a goal that was important to their self-image, and Discus recaptured its position in the professional market. After the creation of the Zoom! system, BriteSmile is the last of Discus's worries: After taking market share away from them for years, Discus purchased the professional portion of the BriteSmile franchise in 2006.

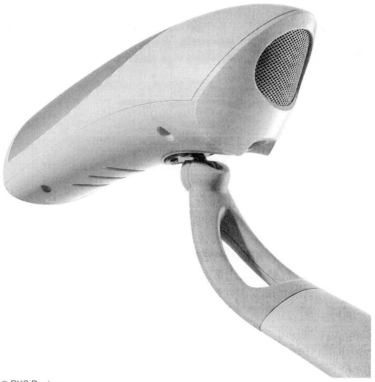

© RKS Design

Figure 6.2   Zoom! whitening lamp and syringe

Finding a Balance

One of the toughest, yet most essential parts of the process is when stakeholders have to come to a decision that they're ready to take their offering to the market. Over the course of innovating, prototyping, and testing, inevitably some trade-offs must be made—either due to time and budget constraints or to preserve the integrity of the offering.

Without Psycho-Aesthetics, these judgments can be gut-wrenching if left to consumer testing alone. But this framework makes us better testers. It enables us to make sure our consumer audience reflects the personas we've built and the market segments we're striving to reach. It also tells us the relevant questions to ask, so we can see if we're achieving the desired connections. Throughout this stage of the process, we can compare the results with our highly targeted goals. This is how we can know when and how well our offering will resonate in the market.

7

Engage Emotionally

To engage emotionally may very well be the holy grail of all business aspiration...that is, with one clarification, we must engage *positively*. In truth, every consumer experience creates an emotional response. And the negative emotions generated by a bad consumer experience can have as much or more impact than the positive ones. The old adage about restaurant patrons holds true. Consumers will tell one person about a good experience and *ten* about a bad one. Technology has only increased this viral effect; a compelling consumer horror story can reach millions of people virtually overnight.

The power of emotion-fueled communication is at the heart of our Psycho-Aesthetics® mantra: "It's not how you feel about the design, it's how it makes you feel about yourself." This guiding principle keeps teams focused on the true cause-and-effect relationship your offerings have with the individuals who interact with them and empowers you to create the positive emotional connections required to generate market leadership.

A beautiful design does not automatically translate into meaningful consumer experiences. Emotional engagement is built through carefully scripted and developed interactions. And the deep understanding of the emotional triggers and unmet desires of your target personas can guide you through the process of bringing a concept to market successfully.

Emotional engagement is the pivotal factor in driving adoption of any new concept, regardless of the industry or facet of life. Fashion, cosmetics, and cars are just a few types of products known for eliciting deep loyalty and emotional attachment. These are areas where consumers have a huge range of choices and view their selections as a means of self-expression. But the relevance of looking at emotional engagement can be understood even more clearly in "forced adoption" settings such as healthcare. The world of medicine offers some of the richest (and perhaps most counterintuitive) examples of design making a huge impact on adoption and compliance and, by extension, long-term health and well-being. The obvious assumption is that nothing is more precious to people than their own lives and those of their loved ones. Logically, adoption would be based almost completely on efficacy and ease of use.

However, nothing could be further from the truth. In segments in which fear is commonplace, unraveling the underlying emotion inherent in the user experience can be the key to driving adoption. The high stakes of health, well-being, and vanity actually amplify this reality rather than diminish it. Design can help both patients and healthcare providers cope with the often tedious and overwhelming task of managing chronic illness. It can also motivate people to address issues that are not life-threatening but the cause of embarrassment and discomfort. Creating empowerment in a setting characterized by anxiety can be a source of sustained competitive advantage. It's one more reason that design and innovation need to deliver both emotional and rational benefits.

The Importance of Belonging

It is difficult to turn on the TV today without seeing an ad for a product related to managing diabetes. In the United States, an estimated 24 million people live with the disease, and the incidence in the global population is expected to grow rapidly. Although many cases of Type 2 can be controlled through medication and lifestyle changes, Type 1 relies on proper dosing of insulin.[1] Through the years, awareness of the disease has increased, but there is still no cure. The consequences of leaving the condition unchecked are dire—blindness, amputation, and even premature death.

In the mid-1990s, any therapy delivering lifesaving insulin in a timely manner represented a huge leap in the management of Type I diabetes. The founders of the MiniMed insulin pump created just such a revolutionary technology. The device had FDA approval, and its effectiveness was not in question. Moreover, the pump was not cumbersome, and it could improve patient lives by giving them more timely treatment while increasing their freedom. Yet, after a few years of initial rapid growth, adoption and compliance tapered off. All the while, the incidence of diabetes kept growing.

A competing (and technologically inferior) product was eroding MiniMed's market share. Executives realized that MiniMed's growth depended on finding a way to increase adoption. The original pump had been designed to communicate its effectiveness and safety; it was housed in a cold, "medical" white plastic that referenced hospitals. MiniMed and RKS created a joint study to identify the problem. To understand the user experience, the designers wore the pump (administering saline) for several days to get at a visceral understanding of what a "Day in the Life" of a real user was like. The verdict was that the pump was reliable and fairly easy to use. But every time the designers used it in public, people would stop and stare. Using the pump in restaurants where it is medically necessary to compensate for food intake was emotionally deflating. The designers realized that this feeling of self-consciousness was potent enough to make people take drastic risks with their health by skipping insulin doses. As this insight was shared with the executive team, a clear mission emerged: Eliminate the social stigma of wearing the pump.

When MiniMed was analyzed alongside the main competitor, we could clearly see why it was capturing the market. It looked less like a medical device and more like a lifestyle product. This explained why patients chose it when it was placed side-by-side with MiniMed's superior product. We needed a design that would allow MiniMed to reconnect with the consumer. Although the mechanical guts of the pump remained intact, the outer appearance went through a radical transformation. Making the device invisible was not possible given the technology at the time. An alternative approach was developed that centered on improving the perception of the device. Pagers were common at the time and even seen as a desirable status symbol. By changing the association from medical device to a cutting-edge mobile communications device, we amplified the perception that the MiniMed was technologically superior and the most durable, reliable, and rugged product. We also created a design that eliminated any stigma and made the users feel empowered.

Due to these Psycho-Aesthetics-driven design decisions, people regardless of age could wear the pump without fear of negative attention. Instead of furtive glances, it served to foster dialogue about managing diabetes. The results were almost immediate. Sales grew from $45 million to $171 million in only 3 years. Shortly thereafter, MiniMed was acquired by Medtronic for $3.8 billion. Medtronic remains the leading maker of insulin pumps today.

Beyond First-Mover Advantage to "First-Connector" Advantage

MiniMed regained its footing when executives understood that innovative technology wasn't all that was needed to get patients to use a device and adjust to all the lifestyle changes required to manage disease. Although the emphasis on innovation has meant that most companies have a robust process for developing new ideas, the embedded belief in "first-mover" advantage can lead companies astray. A more useful frame is the idea of "first-connector" advantage.

When you address the needs of consumers along with the anxiety inherent in adopting something new, an emotional connection can be built. Psycho-Aesthetics is a powerful driver of those connections.

Even with well-designed products, positioning can make the difference between a tepid response and an emotional connection. It is also important to understand *the basis of the connection changes over time.* For example, many tech gadgets sell on the basis of new functions and features when they enter the market. In later stages, they may appeal to consumers because they represent a replacement for several separate devices. Accessories and service may extend the appeal further.

Becoming a first connector requires carefully auditing every touch point and evaluating where the company can do more. Is the packaging difficult to open? Amazon.com formed a consortium of companies to address this issue when it introduced Frustration-Free Packaging. How clear are the receipts? Target receipts are printed to identify items that may be eligible for Flexible Healthcare Spending Accounts (FHSAs). Every consumer wouldn't necessarily know or notice these initiatives. But companies that look at how to help their consumers on such a deep level tend to find ways to connect again and again. Target and Amazon would certainly be well-placed on lists of companies that are trusted, design-centric, *and* high-performance.

The Hero's Journey

The path to empowering consumers depends on you and your ability to guide them past hesitation and doubt and into a rich, inviting series of experiences that leave them feeling great about themselves. To do this, Psycho-Aesthetics employs our interpretation of the Hero's Journey by Joseph Campbell. The Hero's Journey is a classic story-telling narrative used in stories ranging from to Homer's

Odyssey to *Star Wars*. In this methodology, the Hero's Journey is used to frame the process by which consumers bond with the products and experiences they seek out in the marketplace.

Joseph Campbell was an eminent philosopher of the twentieth century, who combined a deep study of both Eastern and Western religion with his knowledge of human psychology, including study with legendary figures such as Sigmund Freud and Carl Jung. His basic premise was that humankind not only needs heroes, but also that individuals can become Heroes through the mastery of their trials and circumstances. He traced the mythic traditions of a range of cultures and identified a set of similarities that were common to all. He famously observed, "I don't think we are looking for the meaning of life. We are looking for the experience of being alive."[2]

Campbell identified three major phases in the mythic traditions around the globe: a) separation/departure, b) initiation, and c) return. Each of these phases has multiple steps, but the cycle involves the Hero being called to action by events around him and first refusing the call before accepting and being drawn into the adventure. Along the way, there are trials, but the Hero receives aid and guidance and ultimately can endure and conquer. The final step is his return to the previous world where he shares his victory and newfound knowledge.

Why We Still Need Heroes

The value of the Hero's Journey stems from the fact that the use of stories is universal and begins at a young age. Stories are the shorthand "headlines" we use—often without thinking about it. They inspire those charged with delivering innovation and the intended audience. Daniel Pink, author of *A Whole New Mind*, highlights some recent efforts at quantifying the impact of stories. If storytelling is assumed to be a component of half of the efforts of professions involving persuasion (such as consulting, counseling, and advertising), its value could approach $1 trillion to the U.S.

economy.[3] He goes on to explain the power of the Story succinctly: "When facts become so widely available and instantly accessible, each one becomes less valuable. What begins to matter more is the ability to place these facts in context and deliver them with *emotional impact*."[4]

In a consumer context, the word "choices" could easily be substituted for the word "facts." It is the job of both the design and its presentation to people to create the context and emotional connection. The urgency to this task is mounting because the design war is often won on nuances—not huge differences in function and price points. Categories such as laptops, which were once driven on memory, speed, and price points are now driven on style, eco-friendliness, battery power, and "touch experience." And they cost less today than they did 20 years ago. Realizing the rewards from design depends on more than a provocative new concept. The execution of ideas must please not only the individual, but also the critics, bloggers, and social networks as well.

The Hero's Journey builds on much of the work that goes into creating personas. Carefully crafted personas can do more than fuel the design process. The stories and narratives that are created can also be leveraged to drive adoption. Today, the story a company tells is often more of an invitation to a dialogue. However, the way choices are framed can change the way people evaluate all offerings in a category. Everyone may not want to drive a hybrid car, but the entire auto industry now needs to have a story about what it is doing to make its products less polluting.

It's the story the consumers remember, and it's also the way that they communicate their experience to family and friends. It provides the reference points that allow us to evaluate our options and reflect on our values. In the most successful cases, we connect emotionally with the company mission or brand and see parallels with our own lives. The Hero's Journey enables the magic of design to be delivered in a way that is predictable, yet still compelling to consumers. It makes our choices feel natural rather than threatening by drawing a parallel between what we know and the unfamiliar. For established categories and brands, the story reminds us of why we should stick to the brand and draws on a bank of shared experience. In both cases, the story amplifies the impact of the design. When deployed effectively, the use of the Hero's Journey can help to articulate the benefits of a new offering, motivate behavior change, and boost memory and recall.[5]

Calling Out the Benefits of a Design

The Hero's Journey is often used to call out the benefits of a design. Although people are enticed by new items, the force of habit must also be taken into account. A good story can help to reframe choices and create new associations by referencing the choices people already make. Many of the concepts rejected because they were "ahead of their time" also lacked a story to call out the benefits and relevance of the offering in a meaningful way.

Motivating Behavior Change

In the case of new products, a story must create a motivation for adopting a new idea. The first cars, after all, were billed as horseless carriages, and zippers were marketed as hookless fasteners to help consumers understand their purpose. The overused idea that "form follows function" in design is often irrelevant in the digital world, as fundamentally new functions are being created. Designers can create cues for new products that reference familiar items (such as the pager look for the insulin pump), but the story is also needed to help motivate behavior change.

Boosting Memory and Recall

In a world of abundant choices, stories can help people to remember the design and why they are making the choice. Simple messages help people make decisions and give them a way to explain their purchases to others. The allure of the Hero's Journey is also about sharing the discovery with others. A shared story creates connections and answers to what writer Rob Walker calls the *Desire Code*: the need of consumers to feel like individuals while also belonging to part of something bigger.[6]

At every stage, it is critical that the experience affirms the qualities and emotions that initially attracted the consumer. Otherwise, the buyer's remorse can also be amplified virally—with disastrous consequences. The Hero's Journey works only when it is attracting attention to features *that actually perform as promised*. The diabetic who no longer feels self-conscious develops deep emotional connections as much as the child who is thrilled with a new toy.

It's critical that you think beyond the purchase decision. The creation of brand evangelists today demands that the "story" includes contributions from the consumer. People are taking a more active role than ever before in seeking out information prior to purchase from a variety of channels, and making them feel like a Heroes at every stage is key to building long-term relationships and dialogue. Everything from packaging, manufacturing methods, customer service, and recycling policies play a role in how our choices make us feel about ourselves. A recent study by McKinsey reported that up to two-thirds of the touch points are actually controlled by the buyer rather than the seller. (Touch points are interactions where consumers learn about a product.)[7] These include information gathered through word-of-mouth, web research, and in-store displays.

Most important, the Hero's Journey does not describe a linear process. It accounts for the hesitation, doubt, and trials that go along with embracing something new and experiencing the satisfaction of conquering those trials. The best designs empower people to take on new challenges. The accompanying stories can whisper encouragement.

The Creation of Heroes

In our adaptation of the Hero's Journey, the stages are broken down to five essentials, beginning with attraction and ending with the creation of viral demand, as shown in Figure 7.1.

© RKS Design

Figure 7.1   The stages of the Hero's Journey

The stages of the Hero's Journey are broken down as follows:

- **Attract**—Attraction is that moment in which we first become aware of something that connects with us. It can be through the scent of cooking wafting through the air outside an eatery, the sight of a crystal clear big screen TV, or an appealing sound that piques curiosity and demands investigation. It can be gained though any or all of the senses.

As we identify and identify *with* our consumers or audience, we can see that the attraction phase of the journey can vary for the different personas. This forces us to develop a palette of attractions that "facilitate" interaction as opposed to "prescribe" it.

It is well understood that creating an initial attraction is essential for any offering. Although attraction was once seen as the goal of design, today it's just the beginning. Furthermore, the channels through which consumers learn about new offerings have expanded rapidly, creating new demands and opportunities for dialog.

Designs that create attraction can change industries far outside their own. Pepsi's famous redesign of its packaging was inspired by the spare aesthetics of the iPod.[8] Dyson vacuum cleaners were initially rejected by many retailers but embraced by consumers who enjoyed both the design *and* the founder's story. Although the high price tag of Dyson products places them out of reach for many consumers, they have powerfully shaped aspirations. As a result, the price points and level of design for entry-level vacuums have risen considerably, and the industry now offers a wide range of colors and features in what was once considered a utility purchase.

- **Engage**—When attracted, your audience responds to the invitation. They touch, smell, or interact in varied ways with the offering...testing to see if the promises made in the attraction phase are kept.

Today, engagement is likely to begin in the home more than a retail setting. Regardless of whether a purchase is made online or in a store, people turn to their computers to learn about what they want. Companies have to create ways to interact and have experiences long before a purchase is made, using methods such as contests, games, special offers, and online tools. In an extreme example of the trend, Volkswagen released its latest marketing campaign for a new car model via an iPhone game.[9]

It is important that the communication in various channels is matched by the store experience as closely as possible. The basis for engagement can be reinforced or lost entirely depending on follow-through. When consumers are happy, they sometimes continue their research and check reviews *after* the purchase to learn more, communicate with other users, or validate their choices.

- **Purchase**—When the buyer reviews the competition, the value proposition should be matchless. The advantage of the Psycho-Aesthetics developed product can make it easy to differentiate between the offerings and make the decision clear.

About 36 percent of people research a purchase online prior to making a decision.[10] Consumers studies also reveal that people will spend from 20 percent to 50 percent more (depending on the category) based on the ratings different products and services received.[11] Despite the research that takes place prior to actual purchases, the experience at the point of purchase can cause up to 40 percent of consumers to change their minds.[12] It's further evidence that the story and design must reinforce each other.

- **Moment of Truth**—The Moment of Truth comes after the purchase, when the consumer interacts with the offering. When it makes the consumer feel empowered, they'll feel compelled to share their experience with others.

By the time someone has completed a purchase, they have already demonstrated their faith in the brand and look to see if their trust is well placed. This is the point in the journey in which people either embrace a brand and become evangelists, or suffer disappointment. The post-purchase experience has a profound effect on future decisions and brand considerations. More important than the design itself is whether it makes the consumer feel as though they made a wise choice, reinforcing a sense of empowerment. Even in cases of "budget" items, comments and reviews reveal that most people have realistic expectations, taking into consideration the price that they paid in their judgments.

- **Heroic Evangelist**—When consumers actively promote their experience, they become evangelists for the brand.

Although much of the research leading to purchases is conducted online, the impact of live conversations still looms large. Eighteen to 24 year olds, for example, use social networking sites more frequently than any other age group (16 percent versus 4 percent), but they're also more likely to rely on conversations with friends and family than other adult age groups (33 percent versus 21 percent).[13]

The creation of Heroic Evangelists is an incredibly complex process, but the payoff is worthwhile: People out there are willing to spread the message for you, less expensively and more credibly. They make suggestions that help you improve your offerings. Seeing the impact on the lives of others inspires your teams to continue innovating.

What It Takes to Make a Hero

Although the steps in the Hero's Journey are the same, the touch points needed to create Heroes must be understood in the context of the category. Although the designs to convey an appropriate message in each quadrant must be created on an individual basis, people are searching for some basic emotions. (Quadrants are depicted in Chapter 3, Figure 3.4.)

Basic Quadrant (Lower Left)

In the Basic quadrant, the Hero's Journey depends on providing reliability and consistency. These qualities need to be conveyed in a short amount of time because the purchase decision is made quickly—and is often driven by price. Although many of these items may be default choices (detergents, household products, and so on) even small interactions that engage the senses can help to motivate change. Touching a product, testing a new scent, or watching a demo increases consumer's sense of ownership and control and can drive adoption. The benefits need to be designed into the product and called out in the packaging. The advantages of the offering need to be visible fairly quickly (for example, that new spot cleaner has to work right away)—because the Hero's Journey tends to be a shorter experience for basic products than any other.

This is in some ways the most exciting and challenging area to work and represents large opportunities. Because the category is driven by volume, and is intensely competitive, products must appeal to a wide variety of personas and perform under more exacting conditions and usage scenarios. Innovations here are difficult but present huge opportunities to create market disruption.

Artistic Quadrant (Upper Left)

Heroes in the artistic quadrant seek out what is unique and different and want to learn more about the tiny details of an offering. Here, extending the attraction phase is important. This person enthusiastically seeks out information on how something was made, for example, or plans for the arrival of a limited edition product or traveling art exhibit.

Here, aesthetics are highly prized—whether it's for a product, service, or experience. Because these preferences are subjective, they often need to be explained to be fully appreciated. The sour taste of an artisanal cheese or cloudy appearance of seeded glass becomes appealing when the process and its value is understood. Exclusivity and bragging rights are also important to the appeal of designs in this quadrant.

Versatile Quadrant (Lower Right)

In the Versatile quadrant, Heroes are created by engaging consumers on an intellectual level and must take them though a series of carefully architected engagements and touch points that convinces them of the design's efficacy. Here, the consumer must feel that his adoption conveys that he is the most educated and informed person on a particular topic. Heroes in this quadrant, notably doctors, teachers, and technicians, seek out the most advanced options available. Many of these products and services are aimed at the professional markets more than the consumer ones.

Reliability, durability, and technological superiority are needed to create Heroes in this quadrant. Professionals may also need assurance that the supporting players can use the product or service effectively, allowing them to focus on a task at hand. Each of these groups must have a set of attractions and touch points that create a rich and fulfilling experience, one that you could bet someone's life on often times, in the case of medical devices. In a simpler example, this is where we can see the experience of an Apple store creates Hero's of its staff and the consumers by creating a highly interactive "Apple experience."

Enriched Quadrant (Upper Right)

The Enriched quadrant consists of aspirational products and experiences meant to signal status and identity such as watches, cars, or travel. When design is used to enhance items from other quadrants and create rich, immersive experience, it may migrate into the Enriched quadrant. For example, a Chanel handbag or a luxury car are more than fashion or transport to those who buy them. These are the purchases that have rich touch points and brand experience, giving the consumer a sense of arrival and self-actualization. Enriched offering are generally the most highly prized by the consumer—these are the things that consumers seek out to reward themselves with.

In the words of Joseph Campbell, "If you want to change the world, you have to change the metaphor." Great companies keep finding a way to change the game and create value. They also need to find the Heroes and stories to help them spread the word.

Winning Through Creating Heroes

Stories have a vital role to play in communicating the benefits of design. They maintain their power when they reinforce our own experience. When there is a clash, people will share their own experience. The emergence of so many new channels for communication has also put some natural limits on the claims that companies can make, and what has emerged in its place is a dialog. And many purchase decisions are guided by our own desires, as much as a desire to share. As Rob Walker sums up, "What the Joneses might think is really, little more than a rationale at best. Because what you are really doing is telling that story to *yourself*."[14]

The importance of Heroes needs to be considered at every stage of the chain in bringing a concept to market. How many Heroes are built through your product or service? To what extent do your dealers, suppliers, and other partners win? Are retailers proud to carry your product or provide your service? Who wins from the association with your company?

Emotional engagement is a key predictor of your company's future growth. Ultimately, Psycho-Aesthetics is not about creating products or experiences alone. It's a methodology for creating Heroic Evangelists. Understanding how to create design that turns consumers into storytellers drives the emotional and viral connections that fuel a company's growth.

The Hero's Journey and the Viral Chain

It used to be that companies focused on word-of-mouth based on common sense and the values of the Golden Rule. Today, however, science can actually provide a quantitative case for business practices that are specifically tailored to create connections and communities. The final stage in the Hero's Journey occurs when the Hero returns to share their learning with the community. Let's look at the power of Heroes in our everyday interactions:

Emotions travel through social networks. A study tracking approximately 5,000 people over 20 years found that happiness can spread through networks, and that our emotions change with those of others in our social networks. If a person who lives within a mile of a good friend becomes happier, the probability that this person's good friend will also become happier increases 15 percent. There is also some evidence that the effects of emotion can reach a third degree of separation. Sadly, Dr. Christakis of Harvard University who discovered the relationship also found a similar pattern with obesity.[15]

Word of mouth is the most powerful marketing. Marketers have long provided incentives and discounts for referrals of friends and family. A clear correlation between positive word of mouth and predictive financial performance has been difficult to demonstrate. However, the Net Promoter Score, which measures the likelihood that someone will recommend your business to others, can now be tied to future growth. Bain analyses shows that, on average, increasing this Net Promoter Score by a dozen points versus competitors' can double a company's growth rate. Here are some NPS scores for top companies: Costco, 79 percent; Amazon, 73 percent; and Southwest Airlines, 51 percent.[16]

The power of social networking. There is no doubt about the power of tweets, blogs, and customer reviews to drive adoption—and defection. However, the magnitude of the web's impact bears repeating. As companies try to track activity on Twitter, there have already been five billion tweets. Some estimates place the number of search queries Google receives at two billion *daily*. And Facebook claims that up to 700,000 social networkers are added each day. Even factoring for any distortions in counting, these numbers are unprecedented.[17]

By creating Heroes, you can supplement your own marketing efforts and add a consumer sales force that propels demand and ideas for further innovation. The more responsive you are, the more likely that word will travel—globally.

8

Reward Your Consumer

Putting It All Together

Eric Barnes' wife, Stacy, was the first to tell him that his habit of taking an old Gatorade bottle filled with water when he went running was a bad idea. "It's a bacteria trap," she warned, "and you don't clean it regularly. Pretty gross." Barnes quickly Googled Stacy's claim and was shocked to learn how fast bacteria began to form. Eager to find an alternative, he visited several sports stores in search of a reusable water bottle and came back empty-handed. All the choices at the time seemed cheap and flimsy or more suited to a camping expedition than to every-day life. However, Eric had never used bottled water before. He didn't feel right about the environmental impact of the shipping and that most empties weren't recycled.

Because Eric had been involved in several entrepreneurial ventures since his days as a work-study student at Princeton, it was only natural that he began to wonder if his conundrum represented an opportunity. He had been reading about companies like Method using design as the basis for reinventing crowded categories such as household products. The spark was lit in his mind: What if he could design a great reusable water bottle? As he discussed the idea with his friend Paul Shustak, a Microsoft executive, Paul too was immediately excited by the idea. They knew that there had to be other people like them who would pay more and help the environment if there were better alternatives available.

Barnes and Shustak continued to research the potential for the water bottle and put together a business plan. When they began to research whom they might collaborate with on the actual design, they spotted *BusinessWeek's* latest Best Product Design issue. On the cover was a photo of a neon green RKS Guitar, which had just won an International Design Excellence Award (IDEA). Barnes and Shustak contacted the firm. It was the first conversation in a dialogue that continues today, as the company, KOR Water, that was created continues to grow and expand.[1]

Greening the Landscape

In many ways, Barnes and Shustak exemplify the changes that are taking place in how companies of all sizes approach innovation. Increasingly, the decisions of entrepreneurs and corporate executives alike are driven by three major priorities:

- **Sustainability**—The green movement has reached critical mass, and initiatives to address these concerns are permeating every business. Eighty-six percent of the Standard & Poor's (S&P) 500 has sustainability websites, and some major corporations began to produce dedicated sustainability reports in 2007.[2] For most new products, sustainability is a requirement at the outset. Many older offerings are being redesigned or removed to comply with new standards and changing consumer expectations. Incorporating sustainability is complex because standards are evolving, for both companies and consumers.

- **Design**—As a response to the abundance of choices in the marketplace, design has emerged as the new differentiator. More than ever before, consumers seek out well-designed, attractive products, which are now available in a variety of price points. The lure of design also appears to carry globally. In a survey by the Design Council in the UK, 16 percent of businesses reported that design topped their list of key success factors. In newer and growing businesses, that number rose to 47 percent.[3]

- **Consumer behavior**—Although demographic studies and consumer surveys will always be important, business decisions are increasingly driven by data on actual behavior—not incomes. Direct consumer observation today can be easily supplemented by visits to websites and blogs, where attitudes and unedited feedback can be accessed at low cost. The reasons for adoption—and the barriers to adoption—can often be uncovered with greater speed and accuracy using these tools.

As Barnes and Shustak mapped out their initial strategy, they describe what they refer to as the "perfect storm"—a crowded market place, where design could make a difference, an still-nascent backlash against bottled water, and concerns about Bisphenol-A (BPA), a chemical used in many reusable water bottles. From their own experience as well as their research, they knew that these trends were converging and creating a new market opportunity.

For the practice of Psycho-Aesthetics®, the KOR challenge presented the "perfect opportunity." It was a chance to look at the convergence of behavior, design, and sustainability and question assumptions about markets, consumers, and creative boundaries. The limited budget of KOR's founders was a test of how well the framework could hold up under intense pressure. It was also a chance to definitively show that individuals could have an impact on the "wicked problems" facing the planet. Design could be the driver that motivated change, to the benefit of the planet and all the stakeholders. It was a chance to start from scratch and rewrite the rules. Could design be used to create not just a product, but also a company and a movement?

Enable Your Stakeholders

Barnes and Shustak brought with them the practical experience of having worked on new product developments in large organizations and were familiar with the process of creating strategy, financial analyses, and market positioning to support new projects. Moreover, both of them had experience with emerging technologies, which involved developing user interfaces and understanding how to drive adoption. Design was something they both had a natural interest in, as well as a clear-cut mission.

Barnes and Shustak came to the project armed with significant market research. Barnes had a clear idea of the market segments he felt were attractive. From his Microsoft days, Shustak knew the persona methodology and many strategic frameworks. Still, they were clear about the benefits of the Psycho-Aesthetics process:

> "When you're as passionate as we were, you really need the structure. You need to be challenged and you need a sanity check. Although we had looked at many different brands that we considered aspirational, you need to have an understanding that goes beyond, 'Apple—great. Motorola—missed the boat.' You really need to understand *why*—from the consumers' point of view. You can derive insight simply from seeing everything lined up—it makes order out of a complex world. We established a rapport with the design team because of the process. We got a great compass, and more importantly, it was easy to hand that compass off to others as they joined us.

> "When you're a new company trying to get the attention of investors and the public, too much text really goes against the grain of a creative environment. There's a cost to making things too complex—you end up being ignored. If you can show a single picture of over a million discarded water bottles, the point gets across very quickly."

Through the process of mapping products and personas, the founders and design team realized that people who sought out reusable bottles had many different motivations. Broadening the appeal of the bottle would create a larger market. After an intense process of debating priorities, three pillars were established that became hallmarks of the KOR brand—health, sustainability, and design. These pillars amplified all the elements of the "perfect storm" and provided clarity throughout the development and design process. They would become the standard against which to measure strategies, materials, branding, vendors, and business partnerships going forward.

Map the Future

For KOR, the task of mapping the future meant looking outside of its category for inspiration. High-end liquor and cosmetics were closely studied to see how the bottles supported an image of quality and individual expression. "We spent a lot of time in all kinds of places from wine stores to Sephora (a cosmetics superstore) looking at perfume bottles to see how craftsmanship played a role in the product...in water, the only example that we saw of note was Voss, which was a disposable water bottle." Voss clearly referenced fashion in the aesthetic of the bottle and gave the consumer a sense of luxury.

The field was wide open, and the founders knew a few things for sure: "We knew that we wanted to innovate in some way; otherwise, what was the point? We really wanted to have some discoverable surprises with the design, even though we weren't sure what those would be at first." And Eric was determined that the bottle be a one-handed operation, so that it was easy to use when exercising and pursuing a healthy lifestyle. Those were the non-negotiable items. It had to look great and create a new super-premium category for water bottles.

Though the goals were clear, the process of how to get there was not. Design was important, but as health and sustainability were added, new categories, brands, and causes were mapped to identify where consumers were exchanging ideas on these issues. A person passionate about sustainability may be drawn to very different brands and offerings than a design aficionado. The design team set about assessing the brands, movements, and products that had credibility in all three pillars and narrowing down how to convey quality to all of them. Achieving balance among the three goals was also paramount. Too "designer" risked appearing superficial. Sustainability alone could be judgmental. Health, of course, remained important, but many other bottles were already in use among fitness and sports enthusiasts. It would be most difficult to break into this segment.

Although water was an issue that both KOR and the designers became more passionate about as the project evolved, there were explicit reasons that they chose to focus on the bottle. With so many large, well-funded players researching and addressing water safety, they knew that they could not make much of an impact there. Instead, they could transform water consumption into a new experience and create a platform to raise awareness of the issues surrounding health and sustainability. Using design to drive adoption was also important because of the message that the founders wanted to communicate: "We wanted the KOR brand to be about optimism, not guilt. We were striving to make it as green as possible, but if someone picks it up just because they like how it looks, that's okay with us. That's still taking a lot of disposable bottles out of the landfill," they reasoned.

Personify Your Consumer

When KOR first began, the founders began with the intent of reaching a segment they knew well: the folks who were a lot like them. Barnes and Shustak recall their initial feelings about the water bottle segment: "What if you're the person who has Kenneth Cole shoes, a Coach bag, and a Blackberry? There was nothing for the segment we like to call the digerati...the urban, global person interested in tech, gadgets, gear, and upwardly mobile career. If you go into a conference room, that backpacker look doesn't translate...."

In addition to the digerati, KOR also had a few other key personas in mind. There were the Machinists—avid exercisers who worked out primarily in the gym and carried water with them. Mothers, traditionally the stewards of the family's health, were another category. The final persona it wanted to appeal to was the consumer looking for "meaningful consumption" who might drive a hybrid car even if she could afford a luxury model. This individual would seek out brands such as Patagonia, despite the cost, because the brand values resonated with her own.

The mapping of personas and creating Day-in-the-Life scenarios provided a reality check on assumptions that were implicitly made about all the target consumers. The personas were significantly refined and additional ones were added. Most of the initial personas were upper-income, but further research and mapping revealed that the concerns KOR was addressing had a much wider audience. The view of the consumer was broadened in terms of income, age, and occupation.

It was clear that the greatest impact KOR could have—both in terms of building market share and helping the environment—would be in terms of convincing those consumers currently using bottled water to switch to a reusable bottle. Consumers switching from another brand to KOR were a much smaller market and a secondary concern. Research had revealed that the use of disposable to reusable bottle usage was 50:1. As a small company, it was a matter of necessity to focus on those seeking meaningful consumption and those who enjoyed design. As Barnes summed up, "People want to do better, but they don't want to do it for less...."

Addressing the issue of sustainability was especially challenging, because of the complexity of consumers and the green movement itself. Standards are still evolving as to what an acceptable carbon footprint is, for example. But it was clear that sustainability was no longer a fringe movement that could be ignored. Piles of plastic water bottles were showing up everywhere, raising the costs of recycling. The public momentum was beginning to build against bottled water but had yet to reach critical mass. The consumers who cared deeply about the issue seemed to apply the mantra of "reduce, reuse, recycle" to all their purchases, even ones that made no environmental claims. Product reviews in a wide variety of categories reflected this. Consider the reviews on Amazon.com for Olay's 14-day Skin Intervention, a beauty product that consists of 14 small, individually packaged tubes of skin cream. Consumers who loved the product had this to say:

> "I would have given this five stars, but this product like most of Olay's has just a shocking amount of packaging. In this day and age most manufacturers have gotten a clue that this is just unacceptable.

> "Another consumer echoes the rave reviews of the product, giving it five stars, but acknowledges the concerns of other reviewers by saying, 'I'll recycle extra as penance.'"[4]

To make matters more complicated, sustainability tended to attract as many people as it repels because of confusing marketing claims and guilt-laden peer interactions. KOR spoke as much about design as sustainability for this very reason: "We wanted to let the consumer know—hey, we're not perfect. Nobody is. We're right there in the confessional with you, trying to figure it all out—what we like, what's good for the planet. There is never any judgment about the reasons why you bought the bottle. We don't have the ultimate equation...." Making the product attractive to those actively seeking green, health, and design was central to broadening the appeal of the product. The emphasis on celebrities and high fashion also receded as the brand gathered momentum.

Own the Opportunity

As awareness of the environmental impact of bottled water usage grew, the reusable water bottle market began to heat up as generic knock-offs of top brands, such as SIGG, jumped into the fray. The trends of personalization and design (carried over from other segments, such as wine) were becoming prevalent. Bottled-water manufacturers had succeeded in connecting hydration and health in consumer's minds, and even those rejecting disposable bottles wanted to maintain a healthy level of water consumption.

As the team derived Key Attractors common among the personas, the idea of seeing the water was critical. Glass was not a practical alternative for everyday use, and the available versions of plastic bottles did not convey quality. Seeing the water elevated in the right vessel would also reinforce the idea that water was precious, just as the perfect wine glass is a symbol of craftsmanship and enhances the enjoyment of wine. The team began to look for ways to use plastic to create both ruggedness and elegance in the design.

It was the pillar of health that provided a window to break through the clutter. Looking at websites and chat rooms, Eric and Paul began to notice consumer concerns surfacing about BPA, an additive in many plastics. As Paul recalls, "There was a point in time where you would just see one or two posts on the websites that we visited regularly. But as we started bookmarking articles that we came across, we really started to see a hockey stick type of pattern with the number of concerns, complaints, and links to scientific research. We knew that this issue was going to be big and that we needed to be proactive...so we were interested in alternatives to polycarbonate right away." The evidence at the time was still being debated, but the concern was real. The team began to look for a plastic that might be BPA-free. However, at the time there were no known alternatives.

Leveraging the strong relationships with Eastman from earlier projects, notably RKS Guitars, the design team received an early, confidential confirmation that a new material was in development. Based on our talks, they opted to engineer it to be BPA-free. Although the team was still working out many details of design and messaging, the decision to wait for the new material was an easy one. It was a matter of upholding the three central values that KOR used to define itself. As the public concern with BPA gathered steam, the dearth of alternatives created a huge opportunity for KOR. The spike in BPA news and restrictions reached critical mass in May/June 2008, just as the KOR ONE was ready to launch.

Work the Design Process

Eric Barnes was unequivocal about the importance of design from the beginning saying, "We knew that if we could think maniacally about how to use design, we could compete against much larger companies. We knew that was the variable that we had to win on." The design team was already inspired by the cause and the founders. Based on the intense Psycho-Aesthetics work that had been done, they achieved an overall shape and form to work from within three months. The elliptical shape made the bottle easier to carry than the traditional round bottles, and the it could also be carried from the top. The aesthetics represented a huge separation from the outdoorsy feel of what was already in the market, and the team felt confident that it had the ability to become iconic. KOR bottles looked at home in a business meeting, a yoga studio, and a variety of urban settings. It was unexpected but aspirational. Barnes hoped it could be like the Aeron chair, which initially separated people but was ultimately catapulted in popularity when designers and architects embraced it. Though the team was excited about the direction of the design right away, there was more work to be done.

The various design elements of the first KOR ONE water bottle (see Figure 8.1) were:

- **Cap**—The hinged cap was designed to be easy to operate with one hand and close so securely it wouldn't leak even if laid flat.
- **Tritan material**—Eastman's BPA-free Tritan material provides a safe and durable alternative to traditional materials It also has superior clarity, resembling glass.
- **Wide mouth**—An extra-wide mouth makes the bottle easy to use from the tap and fridge. It easily accepts full-size ice cubes, and water can be gulped or sipped easily.

- **Elliptical shape/handholds at top**—These form a "frame" for the water to be showcased and make it easier to carry around and hold.

- **Recycling**—In keeping with the aim of sustainability, KOR provides a lifetime policy of taking back bottles for proper recycling when (and if) they have gone past their useful life.

- **KOR stones**—The cap contained a place for an inspirational message and a way to personalize bottles.

© RKS Design

Figure 8.1   The first KOR ONE water bottle

Creating a design that could be operated with one hand that kept the cap tethered to the bottle required trying more than ten different solutions. A cap that screwed onto the bottle could have gone into production far earlier, but the important idea of innovation would have been sacrificed. The team knew that to achieve the desired emotional connection it needed to offer its target personas a better experience. And it knew that the one-handed opening would help create this connection.

As the issue of the cap came to resolution, other ideas had surfaced regarding the appearance and overall feel of the bottle. It was time to look at the personas again, as well as the Key Attractors that were established early on. As the design was held up, the team begun to realize that adding elements might actually make the bottle seem superficial and contrived, thus limiting the audience.

Barnes' decision on when KOR's first offering was ready drew on lessons from mythology as well: "At some point, you don't want to be Icarus flying too close to the sun. There are challenges and trade-offs in reaching too far. As a new company, you also have to have faith that you have to put together a great product, but you're going to get a second chance. The consumer doesn't need to know everything that you thought of; they need to see something inspirational. If there are other ideas, you can put them in your pocket."

Engage Emotionally

The inspiration behind KOR always included the idea of creating a community united by a love of design and concern for the environment and health. The founders saw how the Summer Olympics in 2004 was where people of all different races and ages were beginning to sport the LIVESTRONG wristbands and support a cause. They, too, hoped that their product would spawn the creation of a tribe.

As KOR was looking for a manufacture that would measure up to their SET (Sustainable, Ethical, Transparent) standards, the converging waves of demand (the backlash against bottled water, the power of design in the market, and the BPA issue) continued to build. Then, in the late spring of 2008, the BPA issue reached a tipping point. Canada prohibited the use of plastic containing BPA in baby products, and some cities banned BPA altogether. KOR was still in tooling as one top competitor began to use Tritan material in their bottles. It was a nerve-wracking time. The team was so close; it was frustrating that challenges in manufacturing caused delays. Though it lost the chance to be the first BPA-free reusable water bottle, none of the competitors had the entire package of design, health, and sustainability.

But then KOR hit a roadblock it had failed to anticipate. Like so many small businesses, unanticipated expenses in tooling had emptied its coffers. There was no money left to give the bottle the marketing launch it deserved. It had built a website, but there was the real risk of taking the website live and getting no traffic—the proverbial tree falling in the woods with no one to hear it.

Luckily, the RKS team had recently proven the success of applying the Hero's Journey to marketing strategy. They'd earlier put out a carefully targeted press release about the Mimique cell phone concept (one of the first concepts designed for Google Android), which became an instant Internet hit. The RKS team knew they could generate this same kind of attention for the KOR ONE. It had a product designed to connect emotionally; it had wonderful photography (taken by Ben Dowdy and Carla Olson of Eastman); and it had the timing to capture the raw power of that perfect storm.

When KOR and Eastman saw the results generated by the Mimique press release, they gave RKS the nod to take the lead. RKS customized a list of key blogs created to fit the audience for KOR's offering, ensuring that each target persona would be reached. The team compared notes with KOR to make sure the websites that had provided early insight and inspiration for Eric and Paul were included.

A press release was carefully crafted to ensure that all the emotional touch points of the design were showcased. In mid-June, news of the KOR ONE Hydration Vessel was launched. The response was immediate and overwhelming. News of the KOR ONE was picked up by top sites, including Uncrate, Cool Hunting, Boing Boing, Gizmodo, Yanko, Tree Hugger, Daily Candy, and hundreds more. The results surpassed all expectations—KOR soon found itself oversubscribed for its first year's capacity.

The KOR ONE story continued to spin into mainstream media including top newspapers (*The New York Times*), magazines (Oprah's

O Magazine, *Outside*, *Us Weekly*, *Metropolis*, *Women's Running*), and TV, with appearances on both CBS's "The Early Show" and ABC's "Good Morning America." It was featured in dozens of gift buyer's guides for the 2008 holiday season and landed a coveted spot on Oprah's *O* List. The KOR ONE clearly connected. Individual bloggers picked up the buzz early and continue to praise it. Unboxing videos and reviews on Amazon show heroic-evangelist users spreading the news of the KOR ONE. The viral power of finely targeted emotional connection becomes clear when you realize that the press release was sent to only a *few dozen* websites.

Buoyed by the success of the initial release, KOR could afford to bring in an outside PR firm to help with its promotion efforts. Because KOR ONE generated such extreme consumer interest, it has grown its brand without spending anything on advertising. It doesn't need to. Its heroic evangelists spread the word for them (see Figure 8.2).

© RKS Design

Figure 8.2   Blog posts about KOR ONE

KOR founders and the design team grew their greatest satisfaction from the response of consumers, including ones that they hadn't envisioned as early consumers. As a young company, the founders had thought about how to align with high fashion and celebrities to raise awareness and visibility. The budget didn't allow for the glitzy launch, but a grass-roots movement based on shared values was created. Product reviews showed that people latched on to all the pillars of KOR intuitively. As one reader on a blog commented:

> "My evil consumer side says, 'Have to have it.' My body says, 'Need to get it.' My green side says, 'The earth wants me to have this.'...25–30 bucks? Sold."

Reward the Consumer

"We save the world by being alive ourselves."
—Joseph Campbell

"Better Me, Better World."
—KOR

The final step in the Hero's Journey involves the return of the Hero to the world he has left, and the sharing of hard-won knowledge with those in his community. In the consumer context, the sharing of a great experience has the same effect: It empowers both the consumer and creates a viral connection. Today, the urgency to the global water crisis has only gotten more intense. More celebrities and ordinary citizens are joining forces. Once regarded as an issue in developing countries, water scarcity and safety are now global concerns. Cirque du Soleil founder Guy Laliberté was one of the first civilian space travelers and dedicated his journey to raise awareness of the global water crisis.

KOR, too, found that the reception the design received created a platform for it to do more to support the cause of global water advocacy. After the successful launch of the KOR ONE, a line of three new colors was created along with a campaign empowering consumers to support different causes related to water with the purchase of their selected color (see Figure 8.3). KOR Water did more than achieve success using design to transform a lucrative but stagnant category. It is an illustration of the "triple bottom line" in practice—a business model that takes into account the interests of consumers, the company, and the planet.

© RKS Design

Figure 8.3   KOR ONE causes: Water Advocacy Campaign

The viral demand that was created resulted in retailers requesting the product. The company hired a dedicated force of sales reps to meet the demand from retailers. Based on feedback from consumers and updating the Psycho-Aesthetics Mapping to reflect the changing marketplace, new items are in development.

The heart of these successes depends on deep understanding of the consumer and tapping into the emotions that can inspire them. It requires a reframing of priorities to making the consumer—not the company—the Hero. It requires rethinking design not as veneer but as a reflection of corporate and consumer values.

The challenges of focusing on emotions require some adjustment. But they are worth making. The fortunes of companies can be fragile. The connections with consumers built through design and experience can provide the insight and the audience to drive change and empowerment for all stakeholders. As the experience of KOR demonstrates, any business success is a matter of persistence, taking risks, and increasingly—design.

Throughout the process, looking at the emotional aspect of alternatives—whether it was the choice of materials, the launch, and the design itself—led in a different direction than traditional strategic or financial analyses suggested. In the absence of a framework for understanding consumers' needs and aspirations, it's difficult to imagine that the same decisions would have been made, especially under pressure. Emotions are even more important when companies are venturing into new areas and new markets, "changing the metaphors" of their industries, and addressing global issues once seen as outside the realm of business.

But learning to unravel the needs and aspirations of consumers (a wicked problem in itself) and learning to apply them systematically can make meeting these challenges more visible, and therefore more possible. Over the years, using Psycho-Aesthetics to empower consumers and stakeholders has helped us both in creating innovation and making agonizing decisions. What you know will get you started. What you need to do will become known. The creative process will still be challenging, but more efficient and transparent. Better solutions and new consumers will emerge as a result. They will share your excitement and help tell the story with you. The result is magic—but the process is predictable.

Part II Conclusion

"I called my latest album *26 Letters, 12 Notes,*" musician Dave Mason explained, "because that's all we're ever going to have—those 26 letters in the alphabet and 12 musical notes—at least in the Western world. But no one is suggesting that there aren't great books waiting to be written and great songs yet to be played." The process of design and innovation, too, is about capturing the imagination of your audience, many times using the same building blocks as other players.

Crafting a design strategy doesn't mean that the road ahead will be easy. Chances are, the competition sees the same gaps in the market and is eyeing the same prize. Furthermore, the need for a "win" rarely coincides with large budgets, generous timelines, and an all-star executive team. More often, it begins with anxiety—either because companies sense they are losing ground or because they are unsure of how to capitalize on a potentially big idea. In both cases, design can help companies bridge the gap between what they know and what people want. Turning a design strategy into a business success depends on keeping the emotional insight about consumers and a robust collaborative process alive during the implementation phase. Maximizing the investment in Psycho-Aesthetics® requires the following:

- **Test and update against the maps.** The learning that takes place about products and personas during the design phase needs to be incorporated into the maps over the life of the project. Depending on the length of the development process in your industry, the changes may be significant. As concepts are developed based on the Opportunity Zone, they should be placed back on the maps for evaluation and testing. This allows teams to get a clear idea of the implications of various choices, reducing the threat of diluting new concepts. The focus on the consumer should guide trade-offs.

Where possible, those responsible for executing the design should participate in the research. Too many handoffs can create disconnects in the design discipline as much as any other.

- **Create a connection with the story at each stage.** Today, the story has a role in every step of the innovation process. For executive teams, a clear understanding of why the problem they are working on matters serves as inspiration. Consumers today, faced with an abundance of choices, are buying into a narrative as much as they are purchasing actual products, services, and experiences.

  As teams test different solutions, a connection to the Hero's Journey and story needs to take place. Some of the best-intentioned and designed concepts failed simply because they were not clearly understood. Whether a given approach can deliver the desired emotional payoff is a question that needs to enter into every decision that is made about aesthetics, channels, and other touch points.

- **Understand the execution challenges.** Whether you're part of a large organization or an entrepreneur, the demands of the market require you to produce at a rate of "fast and steady." Great design still has to be delivered with reliable quality and speed (often through multiple channels); otherwise, emotional connections are a moot point. These are also the reasons that simplicity and looking at emotional response are such powerful tools.

- **Design for the future.** Even the best companies miss some big opportunities. Consumers are constantly learning and evolving, however, and design must remain focused on the future.

Today, companies are competing and designing through collaboration. Cole Haan shoes employ Nike Air technology in their walking shoes. Disney is working with Apple to transform its stores. Even discounters like Walmart have embraced organic produce, sustainable store design and trimmed their offerings to provide a more pleasant shopping experience. The challenges of strategy, innovation and design are being addressed in an integrated fashion—often working with firms across industry boundaries.

We can already see the design profession and consumers migrating from products to services and experiences. Businesses and private citizens are turning their attention to new challenges of the planet and society—the so-called "wicked problems" of poverty and sustainability in particular. As we grapple with new questions, the principles of Psycho-Aesthetics become more valuable. Creating meaningful change is not just a matter of the right resources and intentions, but also the right tools.

Helping people to address these issues requires insight into the needs *and* metaphors that matter to them. Understanding how these pieces fit together requires visualization to make sense of the complexity. It can open our minds to what is possible. But as Mark Twain noted, "You can't trust your eyes if your imagination is out of focus." These tools are not an end in itself but a way of exploring new ideas efficiently. They cannot substitute for the skill and passion of the craftsman.

As we apply our efforts to larger challenges, the tough judgment of when we are done has also become more complex. We are no longer done when we have made something that works or produced profits. Psycho-Aesthetics demands that and more. It provides a new litmus test to judge the success of our efforts. We have succeeded when we can answer different questions. Are we empowering people? Are they telling our story with us? Although we've outlined a process, we know from experience that success is a matter of courage as much as methodology. But we do hope that seeing a way to get from insight to empowerment—in effect, having a map—can encourage more people to make the trip.

Afterword

"It's not how you feel about the design or experience; it's how it makes you feel about yourself."

The belief at the core of our philosophy has guided us on a long journey of innovation and discovery. We always knew we wanted to create designs that empowered consumers. As the practice evolved, we realized that the client teams also gained a sense of confidence from seeing their implicit knowledge and market research in one place. There was something about visualizing the competitors, the evolution of consumers, and emerging opportunities in one place that created a shared agenda among all stakeholders—time and time again.

Of course, the market challenges that each client faced were different. But we found that having the Psycho-Aesthetics® tools made the discussion between creative and business leaders proceed smoothly and create a fast feedback loop throughout the design process. Capturing emotional insight was driving a new innovation dynamic. It suddenly became easier to transform consumer insight into strategy and specific design priorities. Over time, we came to view Psycho-Aesthetics as a catalyst for innovation and understood how to use it across a broad spectrum of business challenges.

Perhaps the most exciting development is that the perception of design itself is evolving. Designers are now seen as vibrant and essential partners in innovation and strategy. As we look to the past and future, we see that trying to understand people at every level has enabled us to create in new ways. And in turn, we can see that design is a potent tool that has helped us achieve many different objectives along with our clients. Some of them include:

Reviving brands
Creating new products, services, and environments
Keeping our clients competitive
Designing and building a factory and processes
Incubating new companies
Developing new business models

We hope that Psycho-Aesthetics has provided a new way of thinking and seeing things. We have shared the foundations of our philosophy here and continue to capture our learning with new innovations as we embrace new challenges. We see Psycho-Aesthetics as a self-perpetuating and forever expanding tool meeting the demands of business, social change, and sustainability. Hopefully, now that we've connected with you on this journey, together we can make better designs and achieve better business results. But, why stop there?

We've all been touched by the impact of rising consumer aspirations, and firms of all sizes have to reevaluate their approach to innovation and design. Global markets are characterized by vastly different economic conditions. A typical pharmaceutical company, for example, may be working on cholesterol medications for developed markets and malaria prevention for emerging ones. The differences can be overwhelming if analyzed with demographics and income. But when markets are looked at through the lens of consumer needs, desires, and aspirations, logical solutions emerge. The benefit of clean drinking water in Kenya and organic milk in Connecticut resides in their ability to transform an individual into a hero caring for their family's well-being. Although the realities in these markets differ, the tools to understand individuals need not be. *The challenge today is no longer about delivering the same goods world-wide, but creating the same degree of empowerment and self-affirmation on a global basis.*

Whether people are looking for the means to survive or the meaning of life, we need to understand people so well that we cannot only speak to them, we can speak for them through design, with great clarity and transparency. Motivating behavior change is incredibly complex—whether it's inside a company or in the marketplace. Regardless of the change we seek to create, *beginning* the discussion by taking inventory of emotions and interactions can lead to fundamentally new answers. It can help to translate research into actionable insights or begin a dialogue with a wider audience. Ultimately, we can create an environment for all individuals to take the Hero's Journey and find their own reflections, empowering others as we reach our goals—whether they are for our companies, our planet, or a cause.

To share our journey and learn more about how you can use Psycho-Aesthetics, join us at www.predictablemagic.com.

Endnotes

Introduction

[1] Daniel Pink, *A Whole New Mind: Why Right-Brainers Will Rule the Future* (New York, NY: Riverhead Books, 2005), 103.

Chapter 1

[1] Rajendra S. Sisodia, David B. Wolfe, and Jagdish N. Sheth, *Firms of Endearment: How World-Class Companies Profit from Passion and Purpose* (Upper Saddle River, NJ: Wharton School Publishing, 2007). These and other companies were examined in this study.

[2] John Gerzema and Ed Lebar, *The Brand Bubble* (San Francisco, CA: Jossey-Bass, 2008), 33.

[3] Gerald Zaltman and Lindsay Zaltman, *How Customers Think: Essential Insights into the Mind of the Market* (Boston, MA: Harvard Business School Press, 2003).

[4] Gerzema and Lebar, *The Brand Bubble*, 13.

Chapter 2

[1] Interview with John Herrington conducted January 28, 2009.

[2] John Gerzema and Ed Lebar, *The Brand Bubble: The Looming Crisis in Brand Value and How to Avoid It* (San Francisco, CA: Jossey-Bass, 2008), 33.

[3] J. P. Donlon, "Lafley's Law: If You Want to Win, Become a Game-Changer," ChiefExecutive.net (July/August 2008).

[4] Marty Neumeier, *The Designful Company: How to Build a Culture of Nonstop Innovation* (Berkeley, CA: New Riders, 2008), 2.

[5] Interview with Tom Matano conducted January 21, 2009.

[6] Interview with John Herrington conducted January 28, 2009.

[7] Interview with Tom Matano conducted January 21, 2009.

Design Awards (Amana)

GOOD DESIGN (The Chicago Athenaeum: Museum of Architecture and Design), 2002—Distinctions Refrigerator

Excellence in Design (Appliance Design), 2002—Distinctions Refrigerator

Chapter 3

[1] Lewis P. Carbone and Stephan H. Hackel, "Engineering Customer Experiences," *Marketing Management* Vol. 3, No. 3 (Winter 1994): 1.

[2] Interview with Simon Fleming-Wood conducted June 5, 2009.

[3] Jessica Shambora, "Consumers Flip for Mini Camcorders," CNNMoney.com (January 27, 2009), http://www.benchmark.com/news/sv/2009/01_27_2009.php.

[4] Statistics on Teddy Ruxpin franchise, including sales of toys and books, can be found at http://www.sgco.biz/SGCTeddyRuxpinDevelopment.html.

Design Awards (Teddy Ruxpin)

International Design Excellence Award (IDEA), 1987—Silver

I.D. (International Design Magazine)—Toy Icon of the 1980s

Chapter 4

[1] Interview with Simon Jones of JBL.

[2] Alan Cooper, *The Inmates Are Running the Asylum: Why High Tech Products Drive Us Crazy and How to Restore the Sanity* (Indianapolis, IN: Sams Publishing, 2004).

[3] Maha Atal, "Sustaining the Dream: Steelcase's CEO on Design as a Business Strategy," *BusinessWeek* (October 4, 2007).

[4] Jena McGregor, "Costco's Artful Discounts," *BusinessWeek* (October 20, 2008).

[5] A YouTube clip of Judge Jackson with his EON speakers can be viewed at www.youtube.com/watch?v=2zrR883SGy8.

6 Dutch Boy press release (June 10, 2002).

7 Brooks Barnes, "Disney Expert Uses Science to Draw Boy Viewers," *New York Times* (April 13, 2009).

8 Michael Winerip, "They Feel Your Losses," *New York Times* (April 9, 2009).

Design Awards (JBL EON515 Speakers)

GOOD DESIGN, 2009

Chapter 5

1 Jeremy Horwitz, "Vestalife Ladybug & Element Skateboards Limited Edition Ladybug," iLounge website (March 17, 2008), http://www.ilounge.com/index.php/reviews/entry/vestalife-ladybug-element-skateboards-limited-edition-ladybug/.

2 Robert Longley, "Why Small Businesses Fail: SBA," About.com, http://usgovinfo.about.com/od/smallbusiness/a/whybusfail.htm.

3 Philip Elmer-DeWitt blog posting (June 19, 2008), http://brainstormtech.blogs.fortune.cnn.com/2008/06/19/itunes-store-5-billion-songs-50000-movies-per-day/.

4 Tom Neumayr and Jason Roth, "iTunes Store Top Music Retailer in the US," Apple.com (April 3, 2008), http://www.apple.com/pr/library/2008/04/03itunes.html.

5 Wikipedia, http://en.wikipedia.org/wiki/iPod.

6 Nielsen Wire, "Women More Ravenous for Music Sites," (October 2, 2009), http://blog.nielsen.com/nielsenwire/consumer/women-more-ravenous-for-music-sites/.

7 Mark Penn with E. Kinney Zalesne, *Microtrends: The Small Forces Behind Tomorrow's Big Changes* (New York, NY: Twelve, 2007), 261-265.

8 Claire McCain Miller, "Who's Driving Twitter's Popularity? Not Teens," *New York Times* (August 25, 2009).

9 Jenna Wortham, "Here's a Story, of a Tech-Support Lady...," *New York Times* (October 13, 2009).

10 Gerald Zaltman and Lindsay H. Zaltman, *Marketing Metaphoria: What Deep Metaphors Reveal About the Minds of Consumers* (Boston, MA: Harvard Business School Press, 2008).

Design Awards (Vestalife)

International Consumer Electronics Show (CES) Innovations, 2008—Design and Engineering Award for the Firefly

GOOD DESIGN, 2009—Pi Headphones; Firefly Speaker Dock; Bumblebee, Boa, and Scarab Earbuds

Chapter 6

[1] Excerpted from Harvard Business School case study, "RKS Guitars," 9-507-003 (Rev. June 28, 2007).

[2] Based on RKS research and Harvard Business School case study.

[3] Jon Pareles, "Les Paul, Guitar Innovator, Dies at 94," *New York Times* obituary (August 13, 2009).

[4] Interview with Robert Hayman conducted January 28, 2009.

[5] Veronica McDonald, "Oral Care Sales Keep Sparkling," happi (Household and Personal Products Industry) website, http://www.happi.com/articles/2003/02/oral-care-sales-keep-sparkling.

[6] Ibid.

[7] Ibid.

Design Awards (RKS Guitars)

IDEA, 2005—Silver for "Pop" Series

IDEA, 2005—Silver for Open Architecture Guitar

GOOD DESIGN, 2005—"Pop" series

GOOD DESIGN, 2007—Wave Guitar

CoCreate Design Competition, 2007—Kama Sutra Guitar

Design Awards (Discus Dental Zoom! Lamp)

IDEA, 2003—Bronze

I.D. Magazine, Design Review 2002—Design Distinction

Chapter 7

[1] American Diabetes Association website, http://www.diabetes.org.

[2] Joseph Campbell, *The Hero with A Thousand Faces*, Third Edition (Novato, CA: New World Library, 2008).

[3] Pink, *A Whole New Mind*, 103.

[4] Pink, *A Whole New Mind*, 107.

[5] Reg Harris, "The Hero's Journey as a Learning Schema," (2009), Harrison Communications: Educational Home of the Hero's Journey, http://www.yourheroicjourney.com/Reading%20Room/ArticlesEssays/Schema%20and%20the%20Journey.htm.

[6] Rob Walker, *Buying In: The Secret Dialogue Between What We Buy and Who We Are* (New York, NY: Random House, 2008), 34.

7 David Court, Dave Elzinga, Susan Mulder, and Ole Jorgen Vetvik, "The Consumer Decision Journey," *McKinsey Quarterly* (Number 3, 2009).

8 Burt Helm, "Blowing Up Pepsi," *BusinessWeek* (April 23, 2009).

9 Ben Silverman, "Volkswagen Unveils New Car Through iPhone Game," *videogames.yahoo.com* (October 22, 2009), http://videogames.yahoo.com/events/plugged-in/volkswagen-unveils-new-car-through-iphone-game/1366264.

10 Harris Poll, "How People Make Purchase Decisions: An Update" in The Daily Stat, Harvard Business Review (June 24, 2009), http://web.hbr.org/email/archive/dailystat.php?date=062409.

11 comScore survey cited in Leo Blanco, "Online Consumer Reviews Strongly Affect Offline Buying Behavior," (November 30, 2007), 901am new media news website, http://www.901am.com/2007/online-consumer-reviews-strongly-affect-offline-buying-behavior.html.

12 Court, et al., *McKinsey Quarterly*.

13 Harris Poll, 2009.

14 Rob Walker, *Buying In*, 68.

15 Dan Ariely, "Scientists & Thinkers: Nicholas Christakis," *2009 Time 100* (April 30, 2009), http://www.time.com/time/specials/packages/article/0,28804,1894410_1893209_1893472,00.html.

16 Fred Reichheld, *The Ultimate Question: Driving Good Products and True Growth* (Boston, MA: Harvard Business Press, 2006).

17 Anthony Tjan, "Five Mind-Blowing Web Stats You Should Know," Harvard Business Review blogs (October 28, 2009), http://blogs.hbr.org/tjan/2009/10/five-mindblowing-web-stats-you.html.

Design Awards (MiniMed Insulin Pump)

American Product Excellence (APEX) Award, 1997—507 Insulin Pump

Chapter 8

1 Disclosure: One of the authors, Ravi Sawhney, became a board member of KOR Water following the successful launch of KOR ONE.

2 The Daily Stat, "Reporting Sustainability," Harvard Business Review (November 18, 2008) in "Sustainable Investment Research Analyst Network" (July 2008), www.siran.org.

3 Neumeier, *The Designful Company*, 12.

4 Amazon.com Olay product reviews.

Design Awards (KOR ONE)

GOOD DESIGN, 2008—Hydration Vessel

Spark! Award, 2009—Bronze for Hydration Vessel

CoCreate Design Competition, 2008—Hydration Vessel

Sustainable Living/Environmental Preservation, 2008—1st Place, Urban Sustainable Design

National Geographic Adventure Magazine, **2008**—Must-Have Gear

Bibliography

Ariely, Dan. *Predictably Irrational: The Hidden Forces That Shape Our Decisions*. (New York, NY: HarperCollins, 2008).

Bettencourt, Lance A. and Anthony W. Ulwick. "The Customer-Centered Innovation Map." *Harvard Business Review* (May 2008).

Brown, Tim. *Change By Design: How Design Thinking Transforms Organizations and Inspires Innovation*. (New York, NY: Harper-Collins, 2009).

Brown, Tim. "Design Thinking." *Harvard Business Review* (June 2008).

Brunner, Robert, Stewart Emery, and Russ Hall. *Do You Matter? How Great Design Will Make People Love Your Company*. (Upper Saddle River, NJ: FT Press, 2008).

Campbell, Joseph. *The Hero with A Thousand Faces*, Third Edition (Novato, CA: New World Library, 2008).

Carbone, Lewis P. *Clued In: How to Keep Customers Coming Back Again and Again*. (Upper Saddle River, NJ: FT Press–Prentice Hall, 2004).

Carey, Benedict. "In Battle, Hunches Prove to Be Valuable." *New York Times* (July 28, 2009).

Collins, Jim. *Good to Great: Why Some Companies Make the Leap...and Others Don't*. (New York, NY: HarperCollins, 2001).

Court, David, Dave Elzinga, Susan Mulder, and Ole Jorgen Vetvik. "The Consumer Decision Journey." *McKinsey Quarterly* (Number 3, 2009).

Diller, Steve, Nathan Shedroff, and Darrel Rhea. *Making Meaning: How Successful Businesses Deliver Meaningful Customer Experiences*. (Berkeley, CA: New Riders Press, 2008).

Esslinger, Hartmut. *A Fine Line: How Design Strategies Are Shaping the Future of Business*. (San Francisco, CA: Jossey-Bass, 2009).

Flight, George Biondo. "Yves and Mitch's Excellent Adventure." *BusinessWeek* (June 2, 2008).

George, Michael, James Works, and Kimberly Watson-Hemphill. *Fast Innovation: Achieving Superior Differentiation, Speed to Market, and Increased Profitability*. (New York, NY: McGraw-Hill, 2005).

Gerzema, John and Ed Lebar. *The Brand Bubble: The Looming Crisis in Brand Value and How to Avoid It*. (San Francisco, CA: Jossey-Bass, 2008).

Gilbert, Daniel. *Stumbling on Happiness*. (New York, NY: Vintage Books, 2007).

Gladwell, Malcolm. *Blink: The Power of Thinking Without Thinking*. (New York, NY: Back Bay Books, 2007).

Gladwell, Malcolm. *The Tipping Point: How Little Things Can Make a Big Difference*. (New York, NY: Back Bay Books, 2002).

Hall, Joseph M. and M. Eric Johnson. "When Should a Process Be an Art, Not Science?" *Harvard Business Review* 87:3 (March 2009).

Hamel, Gary. *Leading the Revolution: How to Thrive in Turbulent Times by Making Innovation a Way of Life*. (Boston, MA: Harvard Business School Press, 2002).

Hamel, Gary and C.K. Prahalad. *Competing for the Future*. (Boston, MA: Harvard Business School Press, 1996).

Heath, Chip and Dan Heath. *Made to Stick: Why Some Ideas Survive and Others Die*. (New York, NY: Random House, 2007).

Kelley, Thomas and Johnathan Littman. *The Ten Faces of Innovation: IDEO's Strategies for Defeating the Devil's Advocate and Driving Creativity Throughout Your Organization*. (New York, NY: Doubleday, 2005).

Kim, W. Chan and Renee Mauborgne. *Blue Ocean Strategy: How to Create Uncontested Market Space and Make the Competition Irrelevant*. (Boston, MA: Harvard Business School Press, 2005).

Moskowitz, Howard and Alex Gofman. *Selling Blue Elephants: How to Make Great Products That People Want Before They Even Know They Want Them*. (Upper Saddle River, NJ: Wharton Business School Publishing, 2007).

Neumeier, Marty. *The Designful Company: How to Build a Culture of Nonstop Innovation*. (Berkeley, CA: New Riders, 2008).

Ofek, Elie, Thomas Steenburgh, Michael Norton, and Kerry Herman. "RKS Guitars." Harvard Business School Case Study, 9-507-003 (Rev. June 28, 2007).

Patnaik, Dev. *Wired to Care: How Companies Prosper When They Create Widespread Empathy*. (Upper Saddle River, NJ: FT Press, 2009).

Penn, Mark with E. Kinney Zalesne, *Microtrends: The Small Forces Behind Tomorrow's Big Changes* (New York, NY: Twelve, 2007).

Pink, Daniel. *A Whole New Mind: Why Right-Brainers Will Rule the Future*. (New York, NY: Riverhead Books, 2005).

Prahalad, C.K. and M.S. Krishnan. *The New Age of Innovation: Driving Co-Created Value Through Global Networks*. (New York, NY: McGraw-Hill, 2008).

Prahalad, C.K. and Venkat Ramaswamy. *The Future of Competition: Co-Creating Unique Value with Customers*. (Boston, MA: Harvard Business School Press, 2004).

Rae, Jeneanne. "A Ripe Time for Open Innovation." *BusinessWeek* (March 19, 2008).

Roam, Dan. *The Back of the Napkin: Solving Problems and Selling Ideas with Pictures*. (New York, NY: Portfolio, 2008).

Sawhney, Ravi. "Over-Innovation: A Cautionary Tale." *Fast Company* (June 22, 2009).

Sawhney, Ravi. "The Psycho-Aesthetics Martini." *Innovation* Magazine (Summer 2001).

Sawhney, Ravi. "Why Designers Should Focus on Focus Groups." *Fast Company* (July 8, 2009).

Sawhney, Ravi. "You Are What You Consume." *Design* Magazine (June/July 2002).

Scanlon, Jessica. "A New Model for Green Design." *BusinessWeek* (January 18, 2008).

Sisodia, Rajendra S., David B. Wolfe, and Jagdish N. Sheth. *Firms of Endearment: How World-Class Companies Profit from Passion and Purpose*. (Upper Saddle River, NJ: Wharton Business School Publishing, 2007).

Underhill, Paco. *Why We Buy: The Science of Shopping.* (New York, NY: Simon and Schuster, 1999).

Verganti, Roberto. *Design-Driven Innovation: Changing the Rules of Competition by Radically Innovating What Things Mean.* (Boston, MA: Harvard Business School Press, 2009).

Vossoughi, Sohrab. "Apple: More Than Just a Pretty Face." *BusinessWeek* (January 4, 2008).

Walker, Rob. *Buying In: The Secret Dialogue Between What We Buy and Who We Are.* (New York, NY: Random House, 2008).

Zachary, G. Pascal. "Digital Designers Rediscover Their Hands." *New York Times* (August 17, 2008).

Zaltman, Gerald and Lindsay Zaltman. *How Customers Think: Essential Insights into the Mind of the Market.* (Boston, MA: Harvard Business School Press, 2003).

Zaltman, Gerald and Lindsay Zaltman. *Marketing Metaphoria: What Deep Metaphors Reveal About the Minds of Consumers.* (Boston, MA: Harvard Business School Press, 2008).

INDEX

ℍ Wharton School Publishing

In the face of accelerating turbulence and change, business leaders and policy makers need new ways of thinking to sustain performance and growth.

Wharton School Publishing offers a trusted source for stimulating ideas from thought leaders who provide new mental models to address changes in strategy, management, and finance. We seek out authors from diverse disciplines with a profound understanding of change and its implications. We offer books and tools that help executives respond to the challenge of change.

Every book and management tool we publish meets quality standards set by The Wharton School of the University of Pennsylvania. Each title is reviewed by the Wharton School Publishing Editorial Board before being given Wharton's seal of approval. This ensures that Wharton publications are timely, relevant, important, conceptually sound or empirically based, and implementable.

To fit our readers' learning preferences, Wharton publications are available in multiple formats, including books, audio, and electronic.

To find out more about our books and management tools, visit us at whartonsp.com and Wharton's executive education site, exceed.wharton.upenn.edu.